CHICAGO

ILLINOIS

A PHOTOGRAPHIC PORTRAIT

Photography by Tom Barrat

Narrative by Courtney Pitt

TWIN LIGHTS PUBLISHERS | ROCKPORT, MASSACHUSETTS

Copyright © 2020 by
Twin Lights Publishers, Inc.

All rights reserved. No part of this book may
be reproduced in any form without written
permission of the copyright owners. All images
in this book have been reproduced with the
knowledge and prior consent of the artists
concerned and no responsibility is accepted
by producer, publisher, or printer for any
infringement of copyright or otherwise, arising
from the contents of this publication. Every effort
has been made to ensure that credits accurately
comply with information supplied.

First published in the
United States of America by:

Twin Lights Publishers, Inc.
Rockport, Massachusetts 01966
Telephone: (978) 546-7398
www.twinlightspub.com

ISBN: 978-1-934907-64-1

10 9 8 7 6 5 4 3 2 1

(opposite)
View from the 94th floor of
875 North Michigan Avenue

(frontispiece)
Chicago Skyline

(jacket front)
Chicago River

(jacket back)
Cloud Gate and Eli Bates Fountain

Book design by:
SYP Design & Production, Inc.
www.sypdesign.com

Printed in China

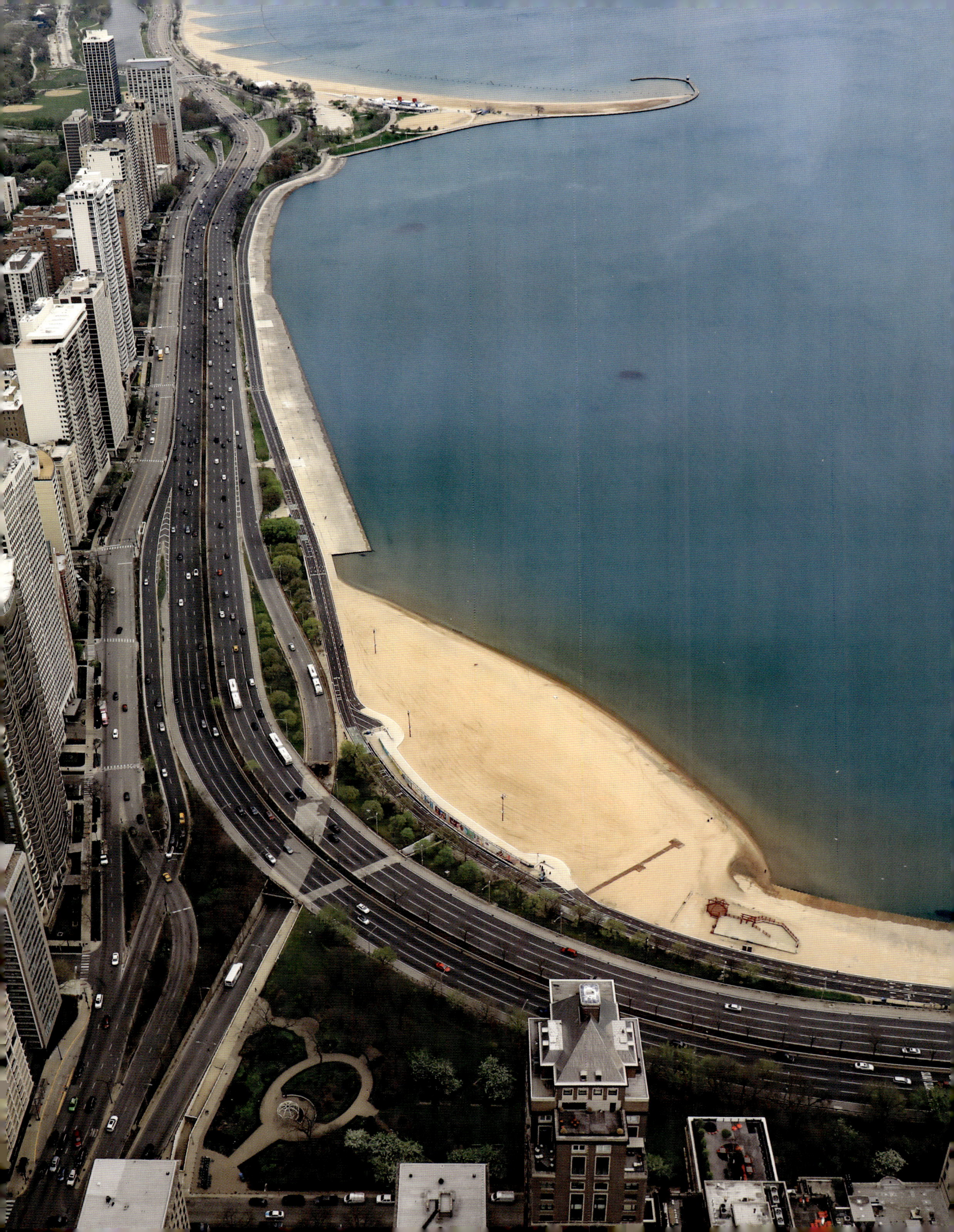

Chicago is one of the most beautiful and desirable cities in the United States. Originally inhabited by Native nations, including the Potawatomi, Illinois, and Miami, Native Americans had formed a vast network of trails, footpaths, and portages. These established routes were essential to early European traders and American settlers, and in the years that followed, this area would grow to a small village, a town, and finally a city. In 1848, when the Illinois and Michigan Canal was constructed and Chicago's first railroad was laid, the city would be hailed as the center for Midwestern trade. By 1865, six railroads had centralized their stockyards on the southern edge of the city. By 1870, the city's number of factories had tripled since the Civil War. Chicago was industrialized.

Then, in two catastrophic days in 1871, the city of Chicago would burn. More than 17,000 buildings, roughly 1/3 of the city, were engulfed in flames, claiming an estimated 300 lives and causing more than 100,000 people to become homeless. The center of Chicago and the heart of the business district were wiped out. Despite the fire, much of the city's infrastructure remained intact, and Chicago would bounce back, reconstructing at record speed. Throughout its rebuilding into a modern city, Chicago would build the world's first skyscraper and see an abundance of unique buildings constructed throughout the downtown area. During this time, the city would experience unprecedented economic development and a population explosion. Just 20 years after the fire, Chicago's population would grow from 300,000 people to over 1 million people.

By the late 1890s, Chicago was choked by this growth, and Lake Michigan, its main source of drinking water, was polluted. In 1900, the city would complete the enormous task of reversing the flow of the Chicago River so that it no longer drained into the lake. This feat would later be hailed a public health and engineering triumph. Nine years later, architects Daniel H. Burnham and Edward P. Bennett would unveil their plan to beautify and improve Chicago's landscape. Over the next several decades, the city would see a widening of its streets, an outer ring of green space created, more public parks established, the creation of harbor facilities, and the reclaiming of the lakefront for the public. Since this initial plan was enacted, Chicago has experienced other beautification efforts, which gave rise to the city being dubbed "The Garden City."

Today, Chicago is an architectural wonderland boasting world-class museums and an internationally recognized planetarium and aquarium. It offers its residents and visitors large open spaces, gardens, pathways, beaches, a pier, and a waterfront with stunning views of the city. From its rich history to its evolution into the third-largest city in the United States, photographer Tom Barrat captures the essence of Chicago through his stunning images. Here is the beauty of Chicago.

Cloud Gate *(opposite)*

Anish Kapoor's *Cloud Gate* was hailed as an "extraordinary art object" upon its unveiling in 2006 at the AT&T Plaza in Millennium Park. Made of 168 polished, stainless-steel plates that reflect Chicago's skyline, "The Bean" is one of the city's most photographed sites, attracting millions of visitors a year.

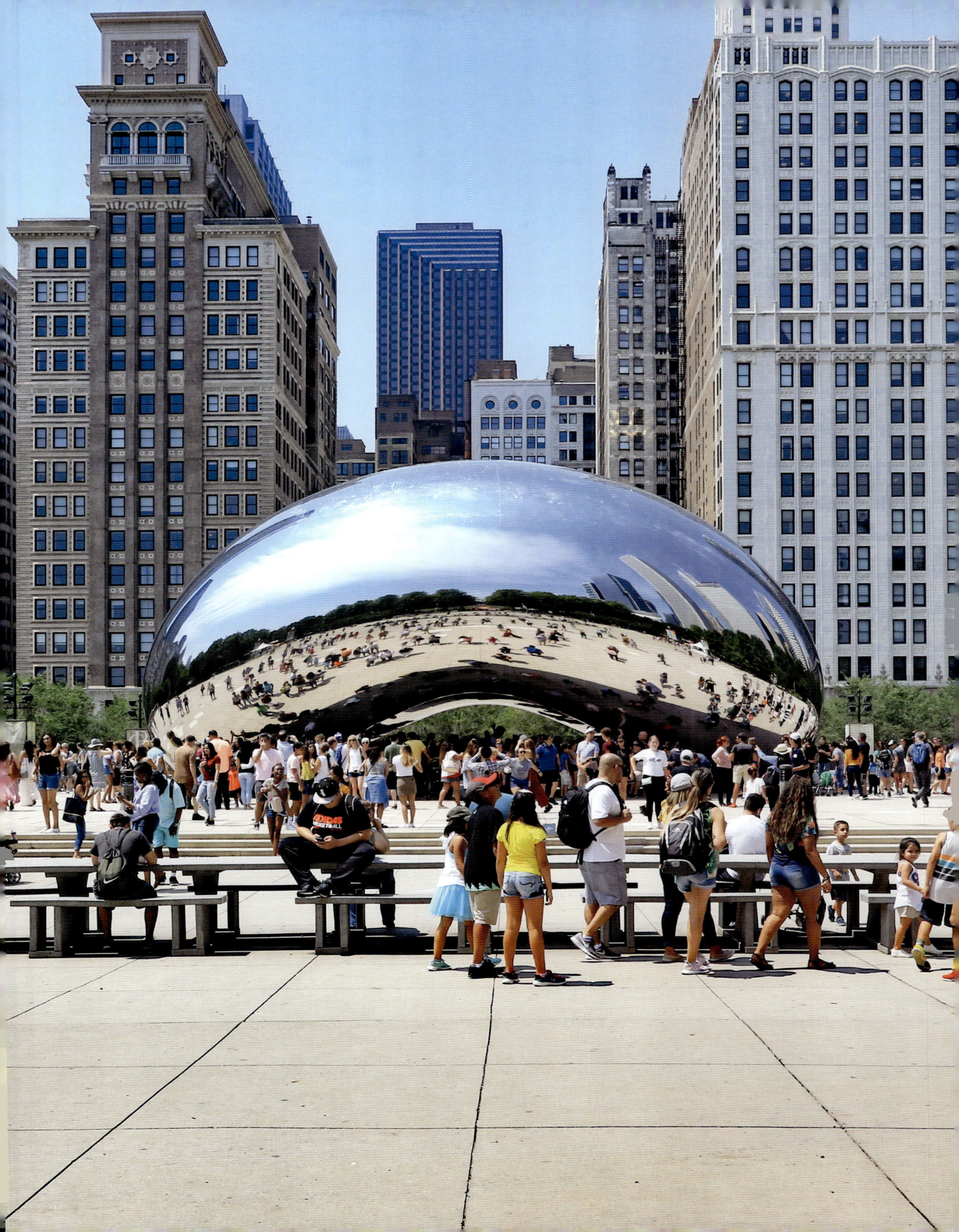

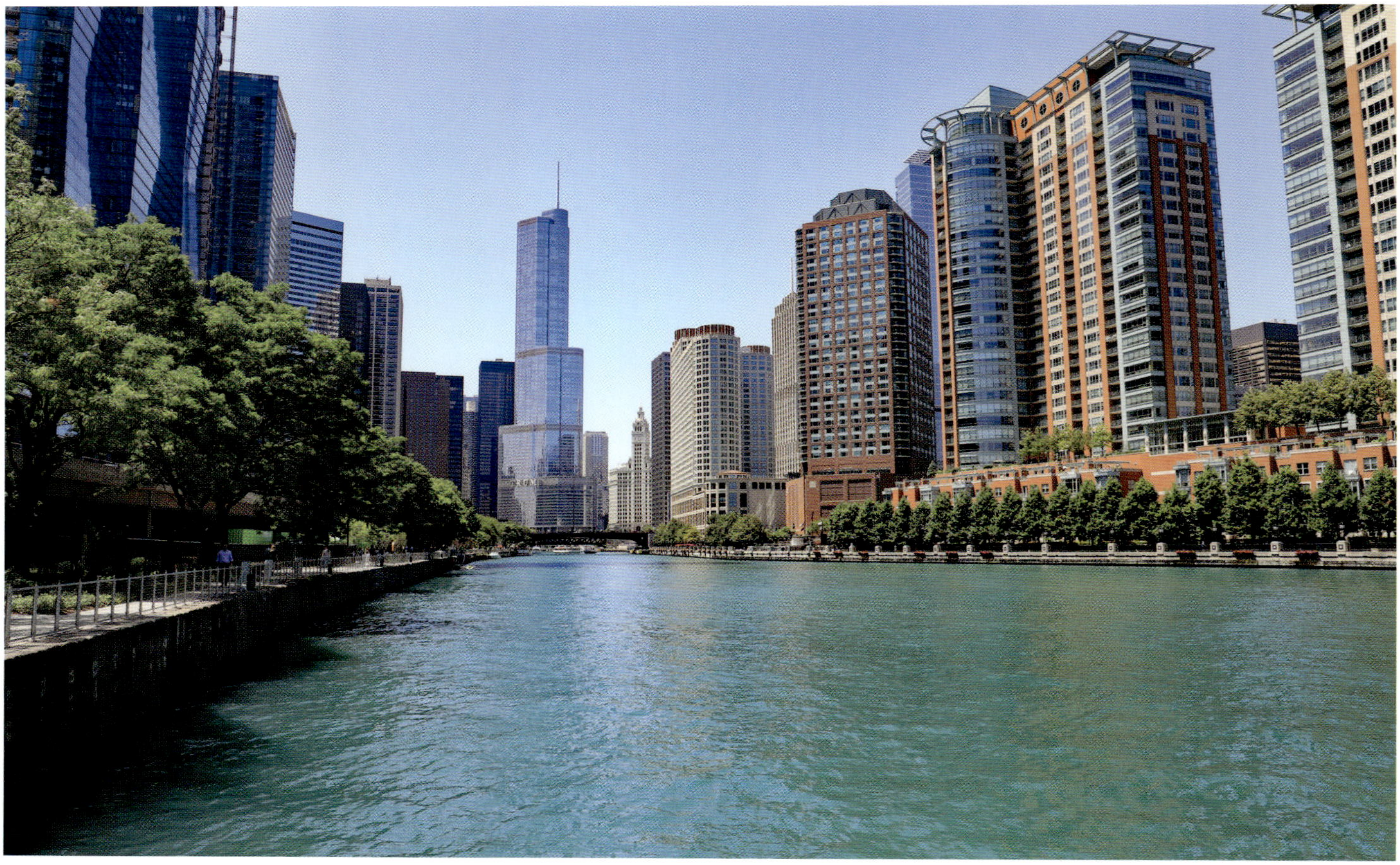

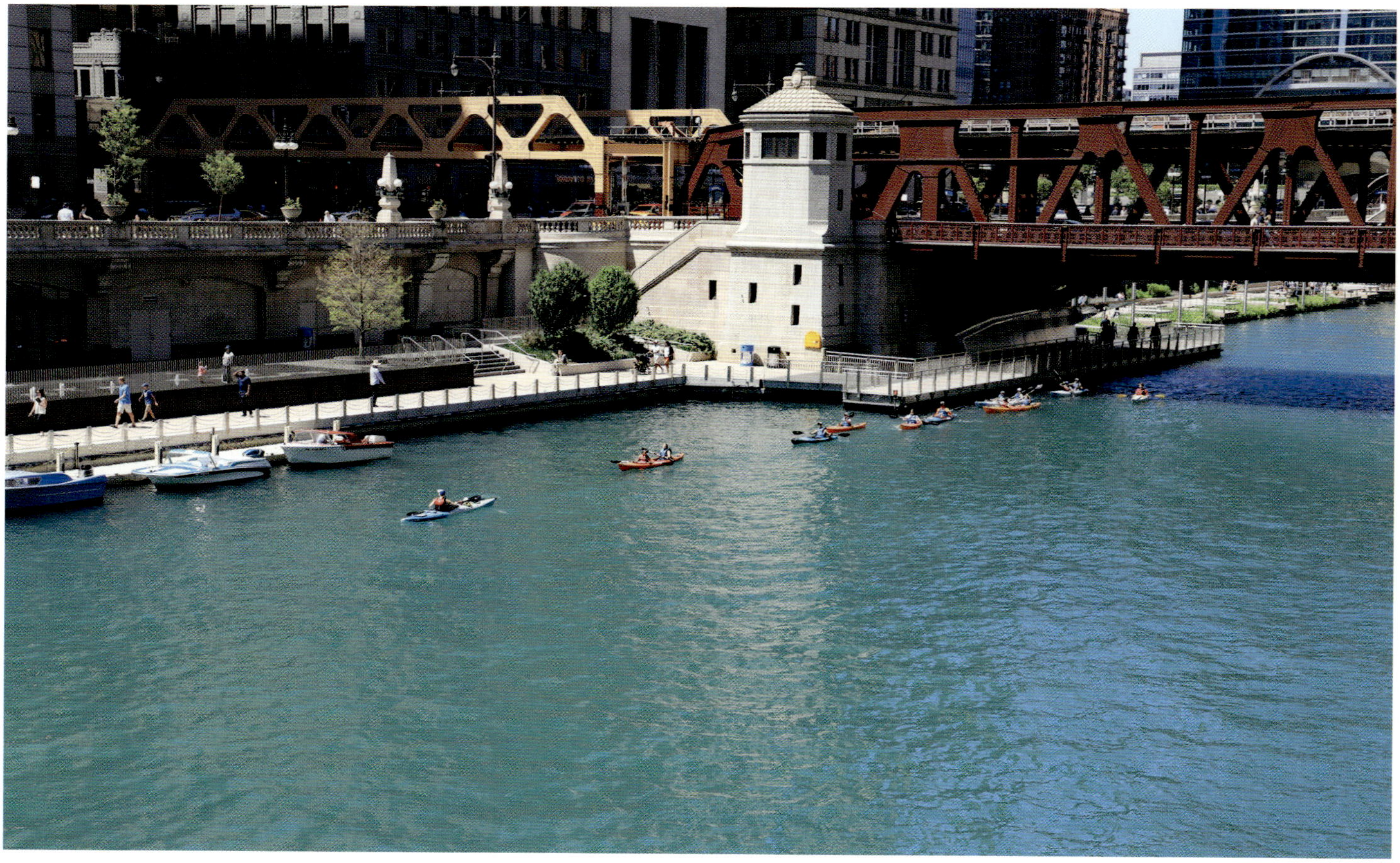

Reid Murdoch Building *(above)*

Facing the Chicago River, this massive, 400,000-square-foot red-brick building, capped with a four-sided clocktower, was constructed in 1914 for grocery giant Reid, Murdoch & Co. In 1945, the company was sold to super conglomerate Consolidated Foods. Designated a Chicago Landmark, today the building is home to restaurants, stores, and office space.

Chicago River
(right and opposite top and bottom)

In 1900, civil engineers completed the enormous task of reversing the flow of the Chicago River so that it no longer drained into Lake Michigan, the city's main source of drinking water. In 1999, it was hailed an engineering triumph and named a "Civil Engineering Monument of the Millennium" by the American Society of Civil Engineers.

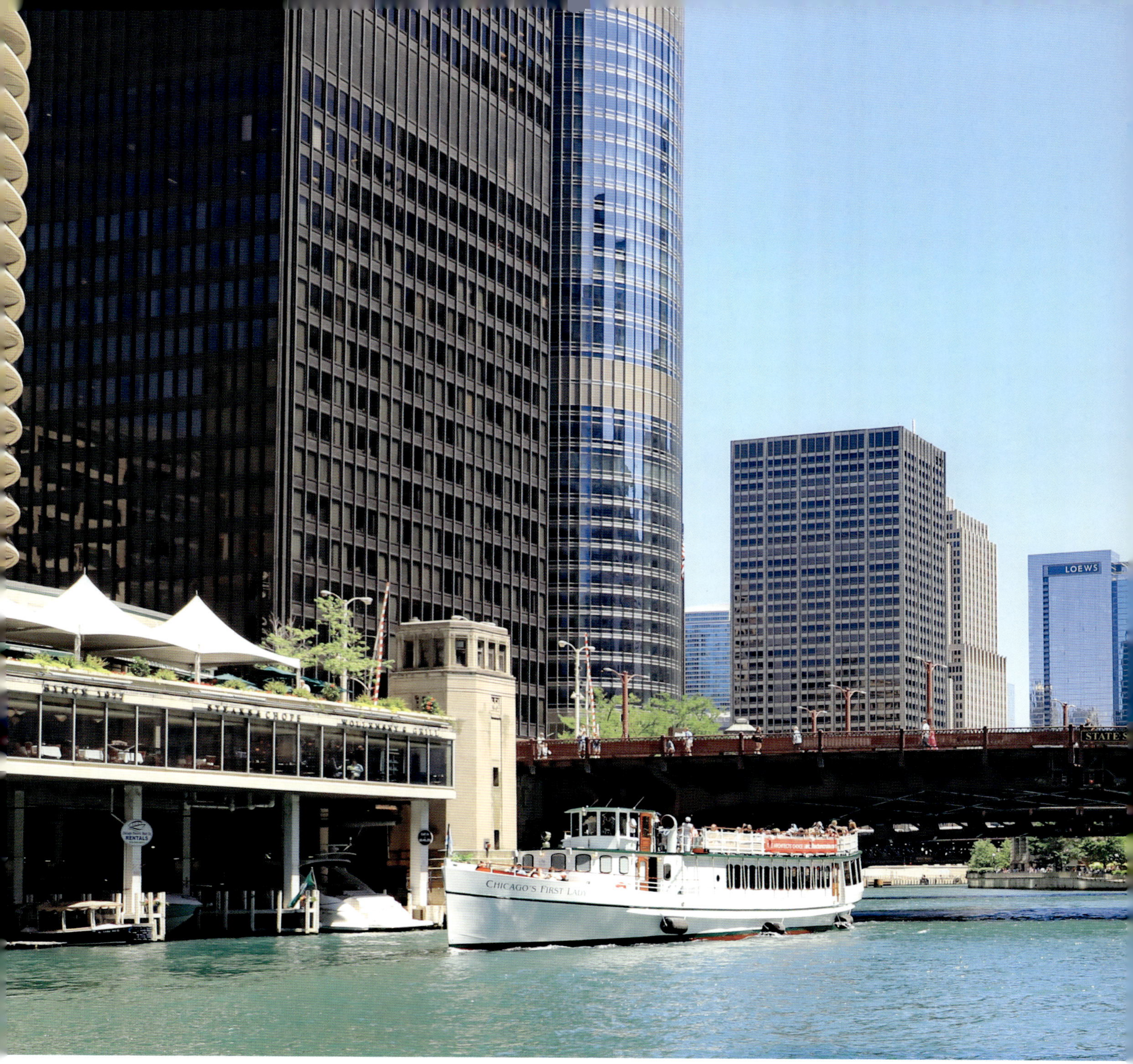
LOEWS
CHICAGO'S FIRST LADY
RENTALS

Chicago River

The Chicago River has been the city's beating heart since Jean Baptiste Point du Sable established a trading post near the mouth of the river in 1779. Today, it is the site of multiple bridges, tour boats, seating, a river walk, world-renowned architecture, restaurants, and more.

Riverwalk *(above and opposite top)*

Located along the Main Branch of the Chicago River, the 1.25 mile-long Riverwalk is a continuous promenade that divides into distinctive areas and incorporates the river's topography. The River Theater's sloped walkway is punctuated with honey locust trees and links the sidewalk to the river.

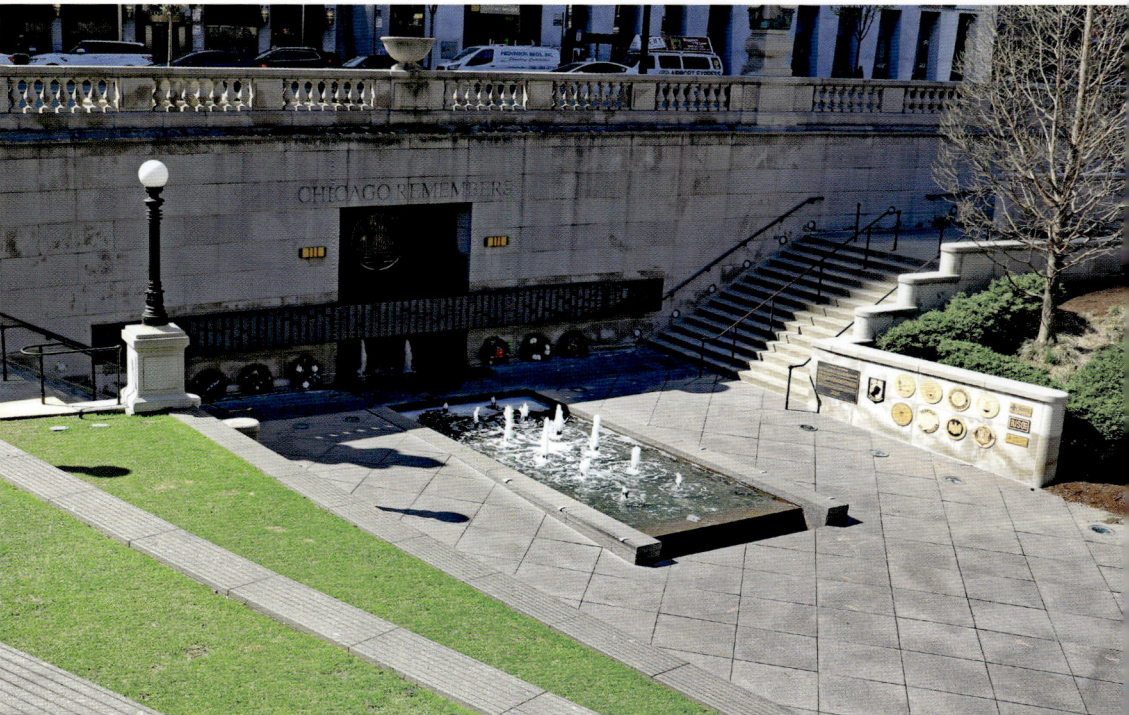

Vietnam Veterans Memorial Plaza *(bottom)*

Steps lead to a small green space and the Vietnam Veterans Memorial Plaza. Located on the Riverwalk and dedicated in 2005, it was designed by Vietnam veteran Gary Tillery. It features a fountain, and a black granite beam etched with the more than 2,900 names of Chicagoans that lost their lives during the war.

DuSable Bridge *(above and left)*

Spanning over Jean Baptiste Point du Sable's homestead site and the site of Fort Dearborn, this historic bridge was completed in 1920 and is a Chicago Landmark. Today, the southwest bridge house is home to the McCormick Bridgehouse & Chicago River Museum, where visitors view the workings of this moveable bridge.

Merchandise Mart Hall of Fame
(above and right)

Eight bronze busts "immortalize outstanding American Merchants," Frank Woolworth, Marshall Field, Aaron Montgomery Ward, Julius Rosenwald, Robert Wood, John Wanamaker, Edward Filene, and George Hartford. Commissioned in 1953 by the Kennedy family's patriarch, Joseph P. Kennedy, the plaza is located across from Merchandise Mart, which was owned by the family for 50 years.

Lake Michigan Frozen
(pages 14–15)

Winters in Chicago are beautiful as Mother Nature has a way of making even the coldest of days bearable with crisp blue skies and breathtaking views of Chicago's skyline. Chicagoans take refuge in the fact that Lake Michigan has never frozen over completely.

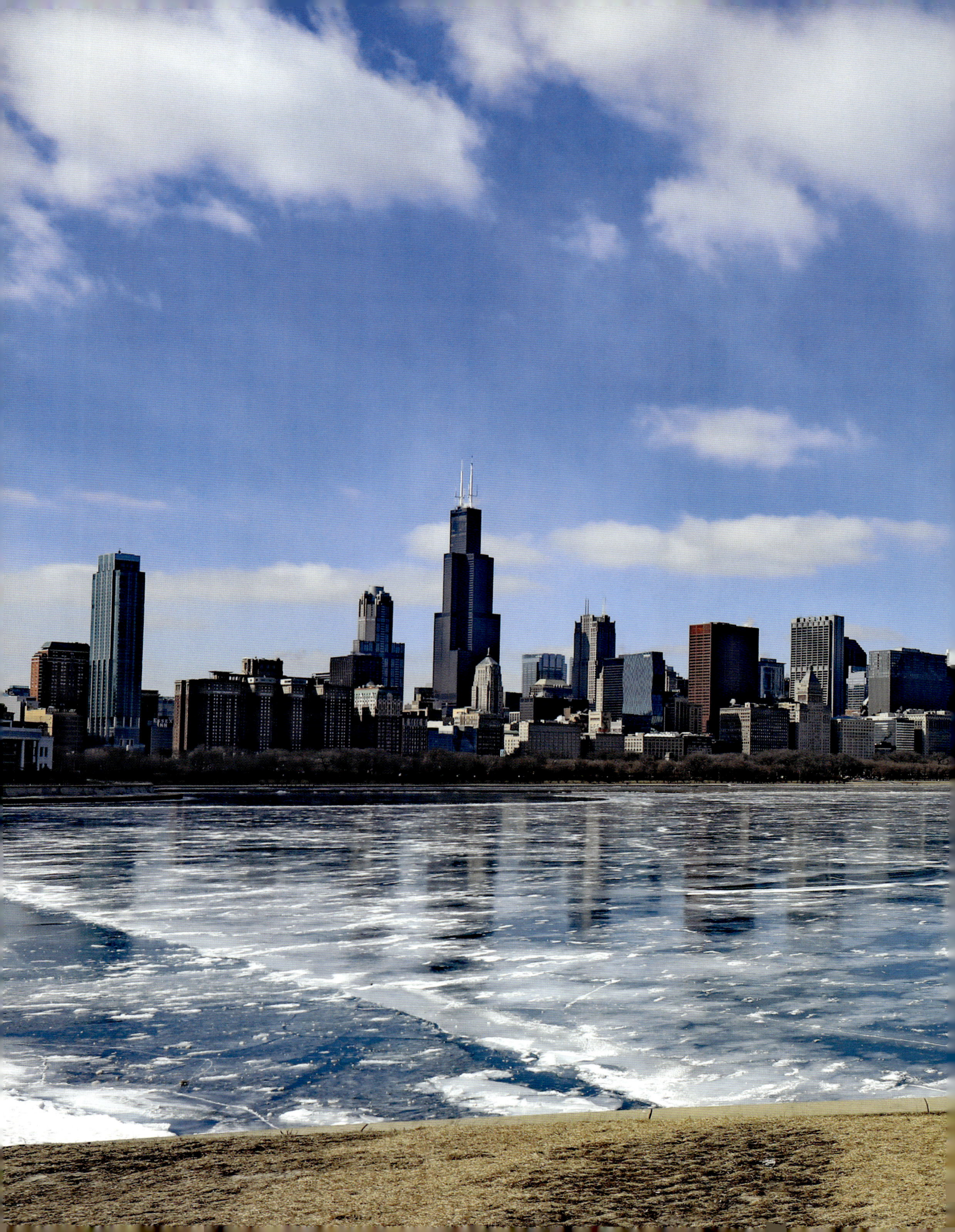

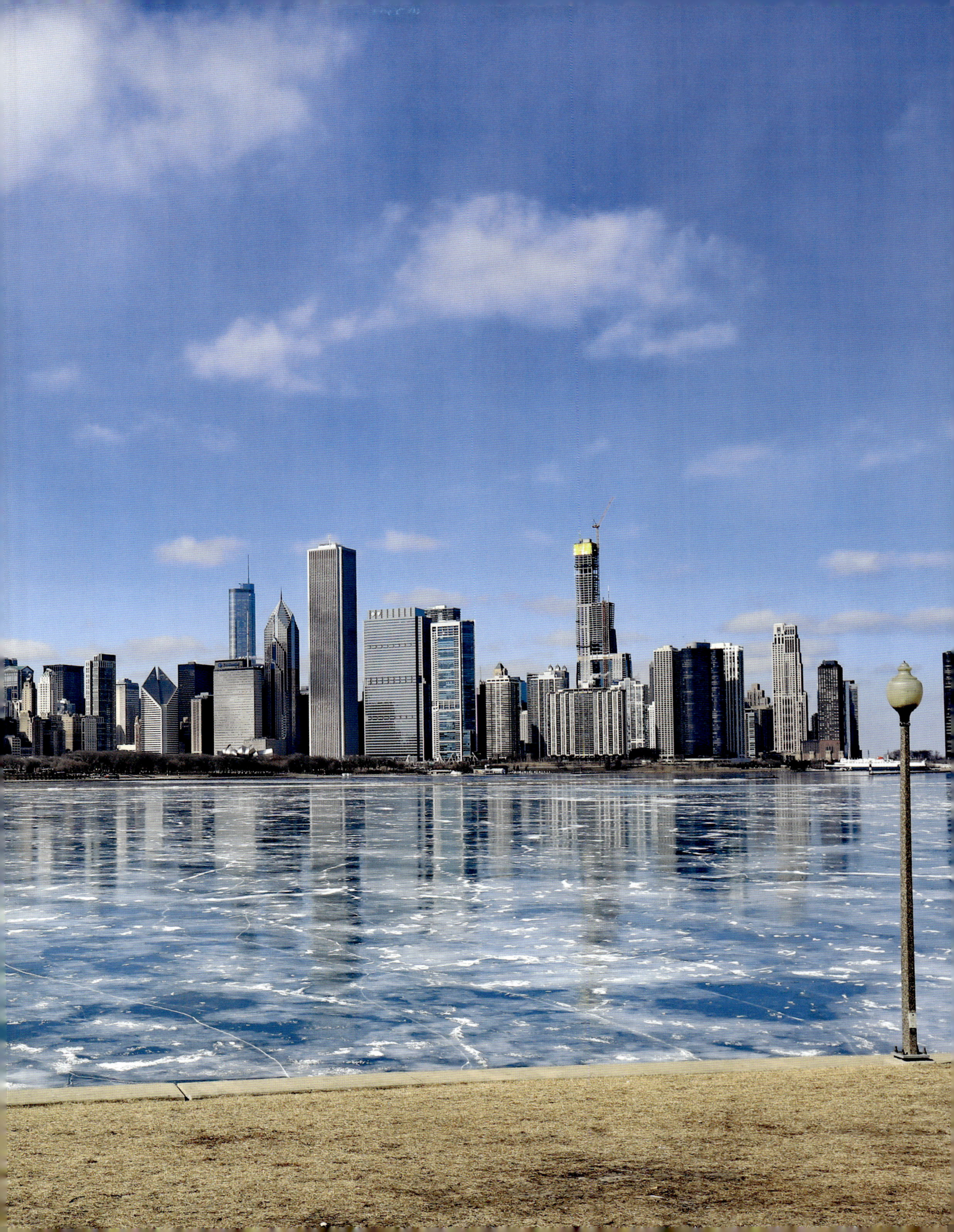

Flamingo

Alexander Calder's open-air sculpture was unveiled in 1974, standing 53-feet tall, allowing visitors to walk under and through it. Painted "Calder red," its overwhelming size is offset amongst the boxy, glass buildings in Federal Plaza. The subject of this stabile, a flamingo, demonstrates Calder's affection for whimsical creatures.

Cloud Gate Sculpture *(top)*

Chicago's evening skyline is reflected in the mirrored surface of The Bean. Selected as the winning designer from 30 potential candidates, Anish Kapoor was inspired by liquid mercury when he created this interactive sculpture. With no visible seams, The Bean reflects, distorts, and elongates the buildings and people around it.

Millennium Park *(bottom)*

Located in Millennium Park, seating at picnic tables and benches near The Bean is available for those who want to linger, rest, chat, or people watch. Encompassing 25 acres in the heart of Chicago, the park is filled with cultural events, art, theater, and more.

Crown Fountain *(above, left, and opposite)*

Two 50-foot-tall illuminated glass towers, united by a black granite reflecting pool, have faces of 1000 Chicagoans that intermittently emerge with a flow of water spouting from their mouths. The pool invokes a feeling of walking on water. Jaume Plensa's interactive video sculpture invites communication, conversation, and play.

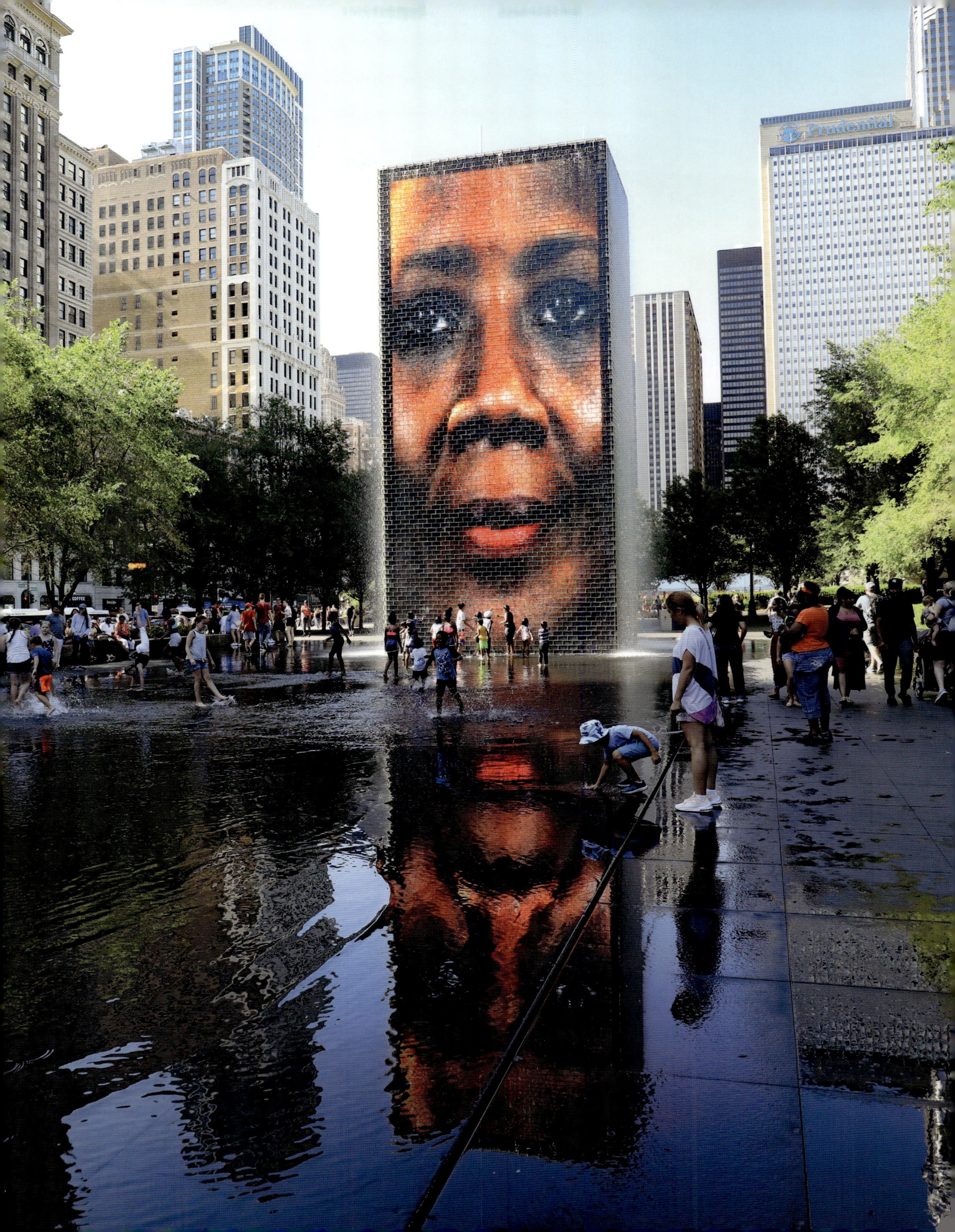
Prudential

Monument with Standing Beast *(above)*

Inspired by a painting series that began in 1962 entitled L'Hourloupe, *Monument with Standing Beast* suggests a standing animal, a tree, a portal, and an architectural structure. Rising 29 feet tall and constructed of fiberglass and epoxy resins, painter and sculptor Jean Dubuffet explained it "as a drawing, extending into space."

Chicago Picasso *(left)*

Standing 50 feet tall in Daley Plaza, Pablo Picasso's untitled sculpture has been a beloved emblematic symbol of the city since 1967. Without an explanation of what the sculpture was intended to represent, Chicagoans have loved debating whether it was inspired by a dog, a baboon, or a woman with a ponytail.

Miró's Chicago *(opposite)*

Chicago's first female mayor, Jane Byrne, fulfilled the city's promise to Picasso that a companion piece of art would be situated nearby his Picasso statue. Funded by the city, private donors, and the artist himself, Spanish artist Joan Miró, at 88-years-old, created this mixture of cubism, surrealism, and folk art.

21

Petrillo Music Shell *(top)*

Commissioned in 1931 to raise Chicagoans' spirits with free concerts during the depression, the Petrillo Music Shell is home to the Chicago Blues Festival, Lollapalooza, and the Chicago Jazz Festival. Named after the 1922-1962 president of the Chicago Federation of Musicians, the bandshell and its seating occupies a block.

Divvy Bikes *(bottom)*

Divvy, a reference to "divvy it up," is Chicago's first large-scale bike-sharing program. The brainchild of then-Mayor Richard Daley, the bikes were rolled out in 2013 as a public transportation option as well as a riding experience for tourists. The program offers 6,000 bikes and 580 docking stations across the city.

BP Pedestrian Bridge

Connecting Millennium Park to the lakeside of Grant Park, Frank Gehry's BP Pedestrian Bridge compliments neighboring Pritzker Pavilion. Constructed of stainless steel plates, the bridge's scaly, serpentine form creates a sound barrier from the traffic below. Dedicated in 2004, at 935 feet, it is a prominent downtown structure.

Jay Pritzker Pavilion *(top)*

A focal point of Millennium Park, Frank Gehry's premier amphitheater is clad in billowing, stainless-steel panels, and offers seating for 4,000 people. Its trellis was formed from curved steel pipes that support a sound system that distributes sound over both the fixed and lawn seating. The lawn seats 7,000 people.

Lurie Garden *(bottom)*

A watery surface and a boardwalk separate Lurie Garden's Dark and Light Plates. Designer Piet Oudolf uses dramatic lighting and unexpected planting choices to bring the "Urbs in Horto" (City in a Garden) to life. Located in the heart of Millennium Park, it is beloved for its cooling water and peaceful surroundings.

Batcolumn *(opposite)*

Inspired by Chicago's skyscrapers, chimney stacks, and construction cranes, pop artist Claes Oldenburg's 1977 lattice-shell baseball bat sculpture stands nearly 100 feet tall. It is a network of 24 vertical and 1608 connecting struts of steel and aluminum. This two-baseball team city has grown to adore this piece of art.

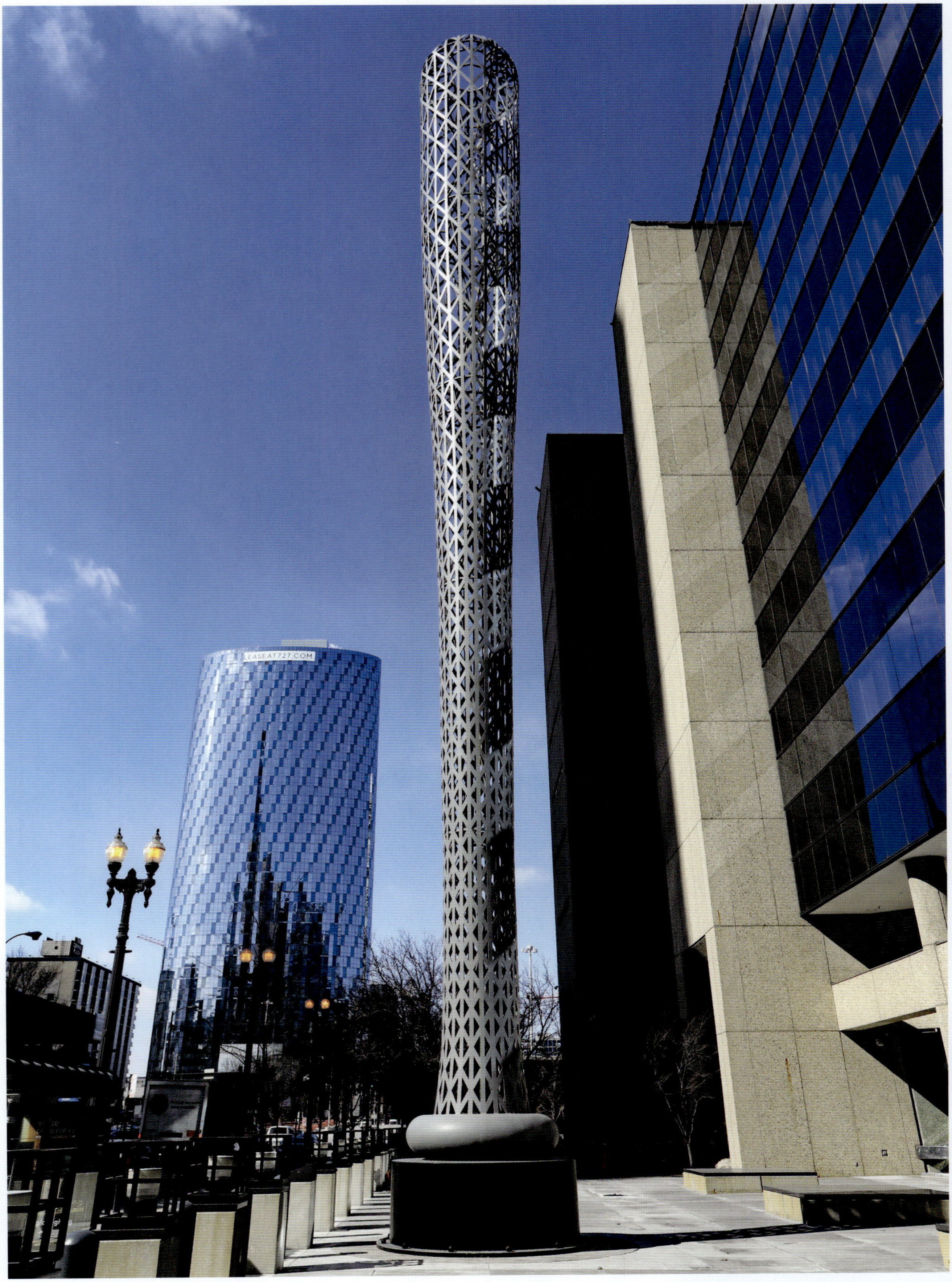
LEASEAT727.COM

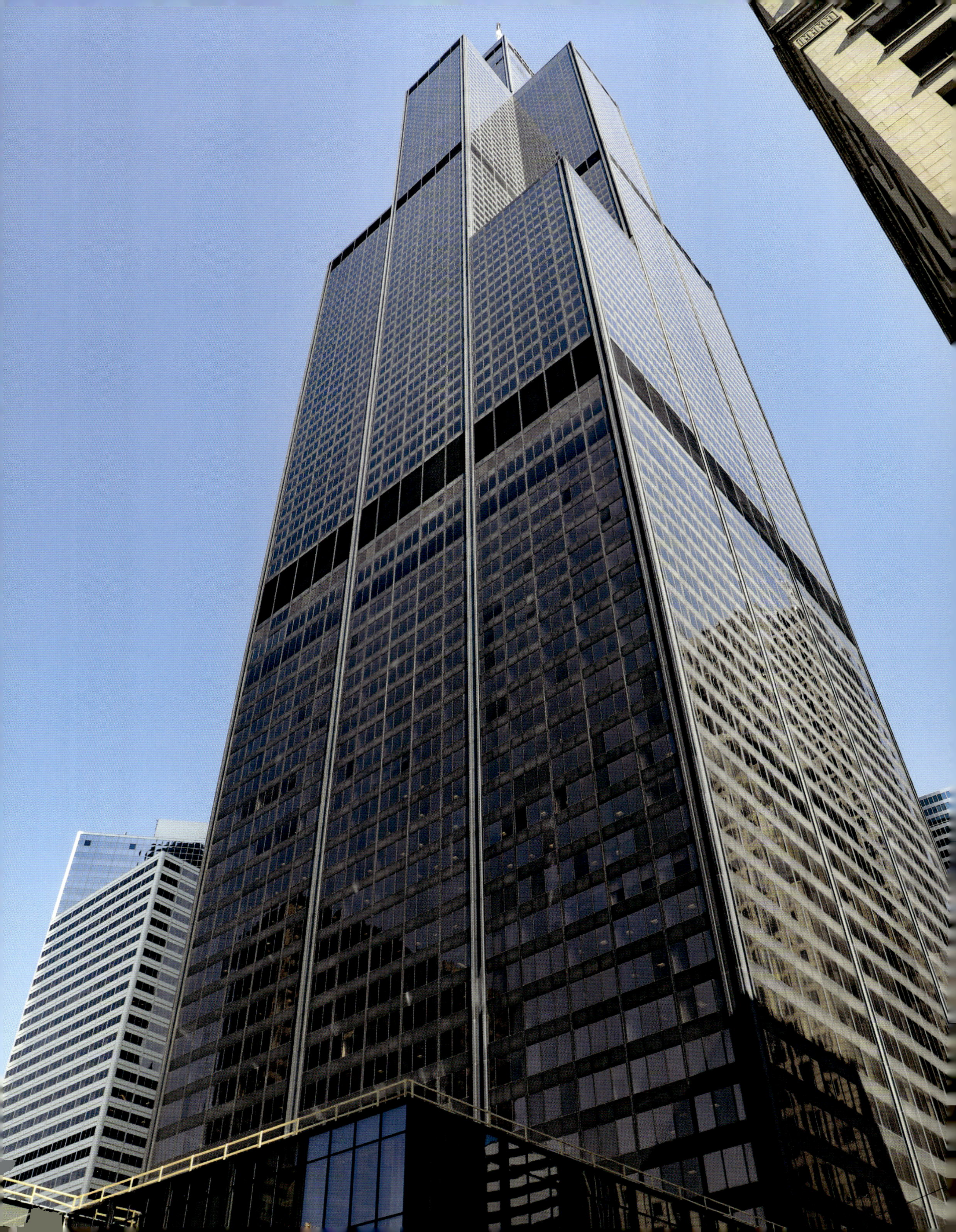

Willis Tower *(top and opposite)*

Sears, Roebuck & Company completed their new headquarters in 1973 with what would be the tallest building in the world at the time. The building is sheathed in black aluminum, with nine separate "tubes" that are planted together in a unifying square. In 1988, Sears moved out of the building. It was renamed in 2009.

Willis Tower's Skydeck *(bottom)*

Extending 1,353 feet above Wacker Drive, Skydeck's elevators reach the 103rd floor in just 60 seconds. It is the highest observation deck in the United States and offers panoramic views of Chicago, including Millennium Park. A retractable glass ledge, dubbed "The Ledge," extends four feet, allowing visitors a view of the street below.

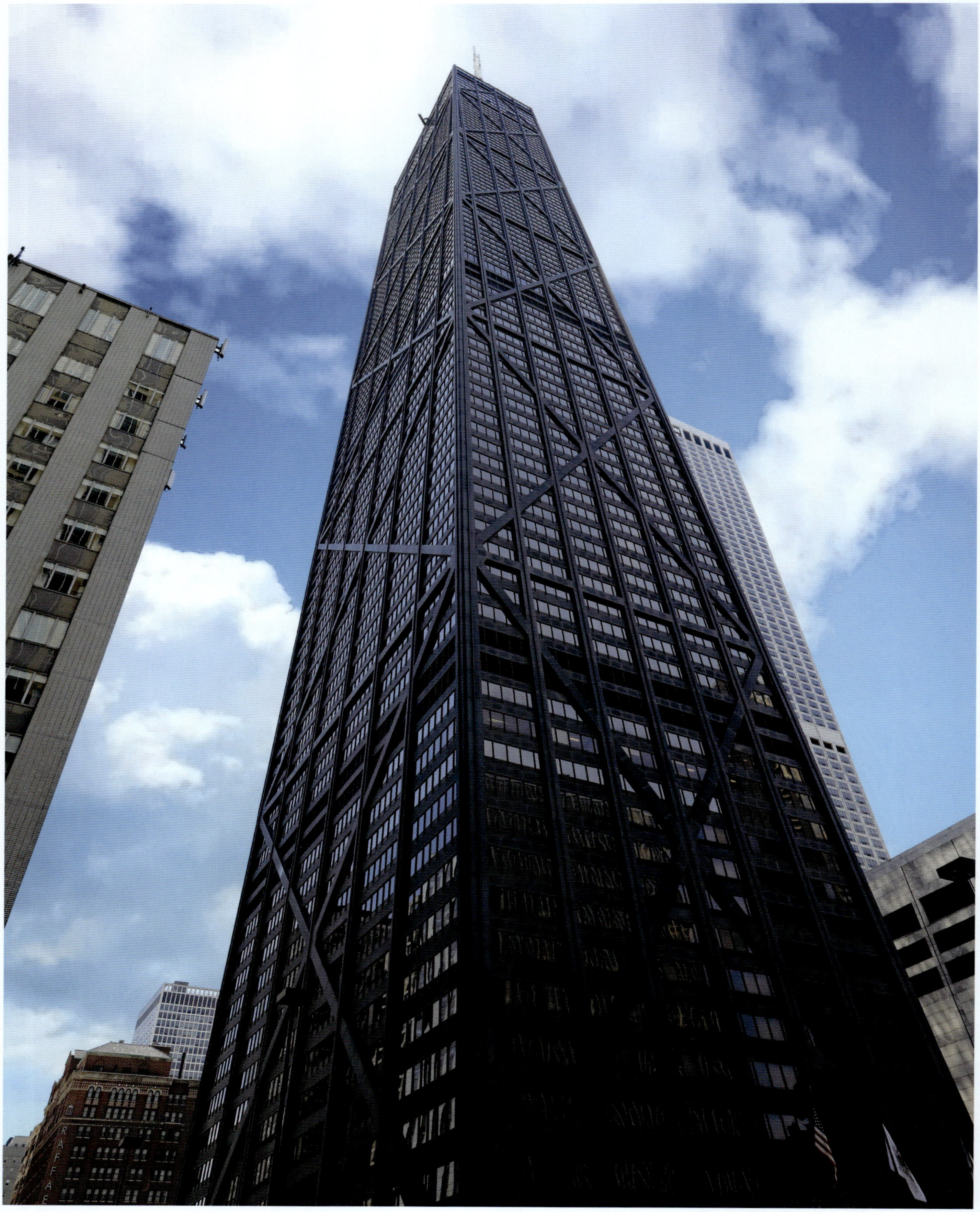

875 North Michigan Avenue *(opposite)*

Completed in 1969, iconic 875 North Michigan Avenue's most notable feature is its 18-story-tall cross braces, which allow the building to withstand high winds. This 100-story skyscraper is comprised of office space, high-end retail stores, exclusive dining, and luxury apartments, and is located off the Magnificent Mile.

360 Chicago Observation Deck *(top and bottom)*

Located 1,000 feet above Michigan Avenue, the 360 Chicago Observation Deck offers breathtaking, 360-degree views of Chicago and Lake Michigan. It is home to Chicago's highest thrill ride, *Tilt*, a movable, glass-enclosed platform that tilts visitors 30 degrees over the city from the 94th floor.

Marina City Towers *(above and left)*

Opened in 1968 on the Chicago River, the 65-story twin concrete towers with scalloped balconies are the definition of Mid-Century Modern. The complex was built to be a "city within a city" and includes large rounded balconies, luxury amenities, a marina, a bowling alley, and the House of Blues concert hall.

Chicago Stock Exchange Arch *(above)*

In the late 1960s, many of Chicago's historic buildings were torn down to make way for the skyscrapers of today. The Chicago Stock Exchange, designed by Louis Sullivan in 1893, was no exception. Today, a reconstructed Trading Room is within the Art Institute of Chicago, and the Arch is on its grounds.

Wrigley Building *(right)*

A favorite highlight of the Chicago River Architecture Tour is the Wrigley Building, which is sheathed with 250,000 terra-cotta tiles that vary in subtly different shades. Completed in 1924 as the headquarters for chewing gum giant Wrigley Company, the building is topped with its distinctive, four-sided clock tower.

Michigan Avenue *(above and left)*

Four stone reliefs adorn the DuSable Bridge's two tender houses. They depict pivotal moments in Chicago's history, including *Defense*, a sculpture that commemorates the Battle of Fort Dearborn. Michigan Avenue is home to the Chicago Water Tower, the Art Institute of Chicago, Millennium Park, the Magnificent Mile, and the tradition of thousands of tulip plantings.

Chicago Water Tower & City Gallery *(opposite)*

One of just a few structures that survived the Great Chicago Fire, the ornate Chicago Water Tower was built for the city's municipal water system. Today, it is managed by the Department of Cultural Affairs and showcases City Gallery, which features local photographers and artists.

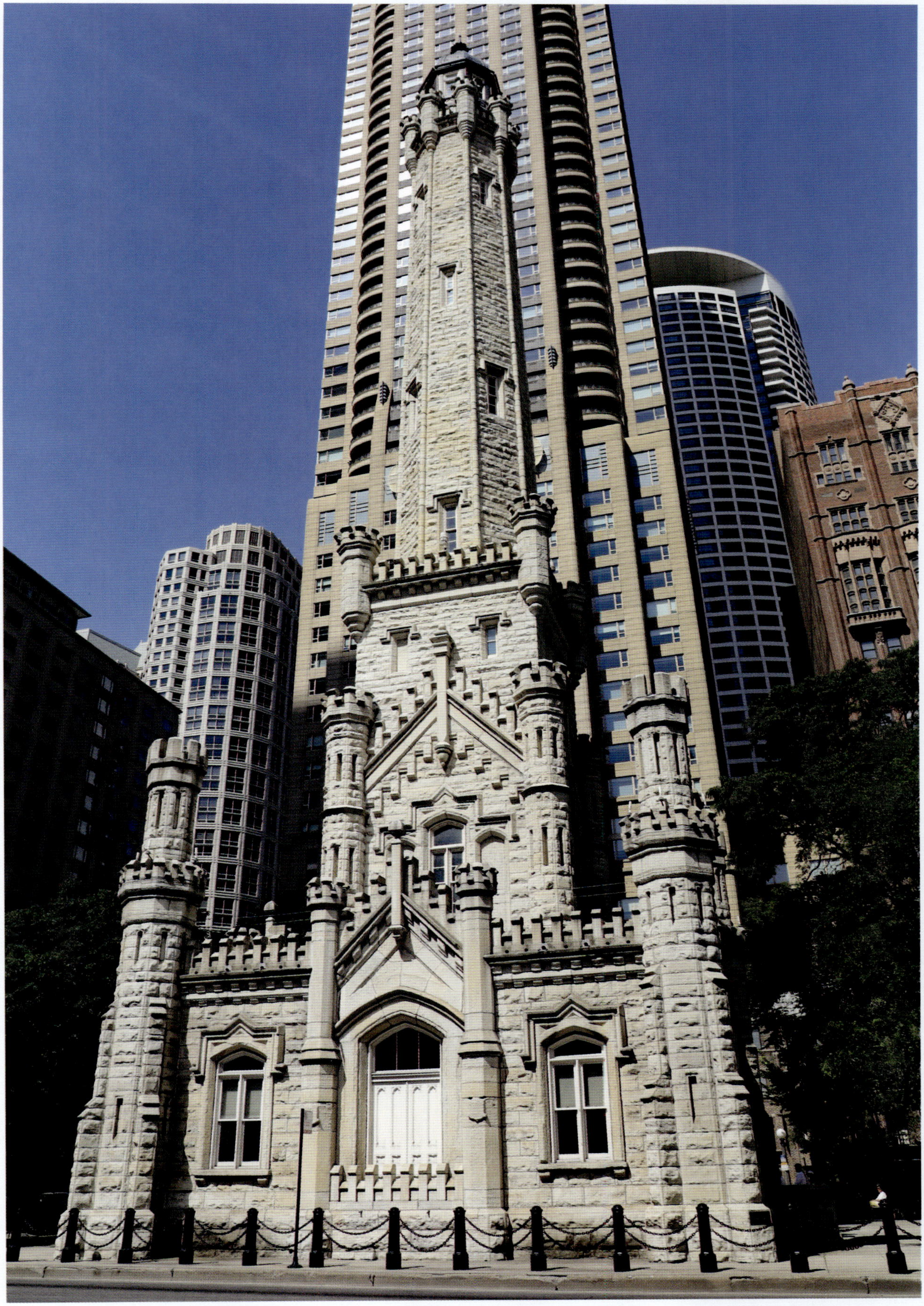

Magnificent Mile *(above and opposite)*

The Magnificent Mile comprises the 13-block stretch of North Michigan Avenue that runs from the banks of the Chicago River to Oak Street. Shaking off Chicago's winter, North Michigan Avenue comes alive in mid-to-late April when 100,000 tulips bloom. At the end of their flowering cycle, the beds are replaced with summer displays.

35

Fourth Presbyterian Church

(above and opposite)

Completed in 1914, the Fourth Presbyterian Church was designed by American Gothic Revival architect Ralph Adams Cram. It is one of the oldest surviving structures on North Michigan Avenue. Made from Indiana limestone, it features a carved stone entrance, arched windows, and a decorative steeple.

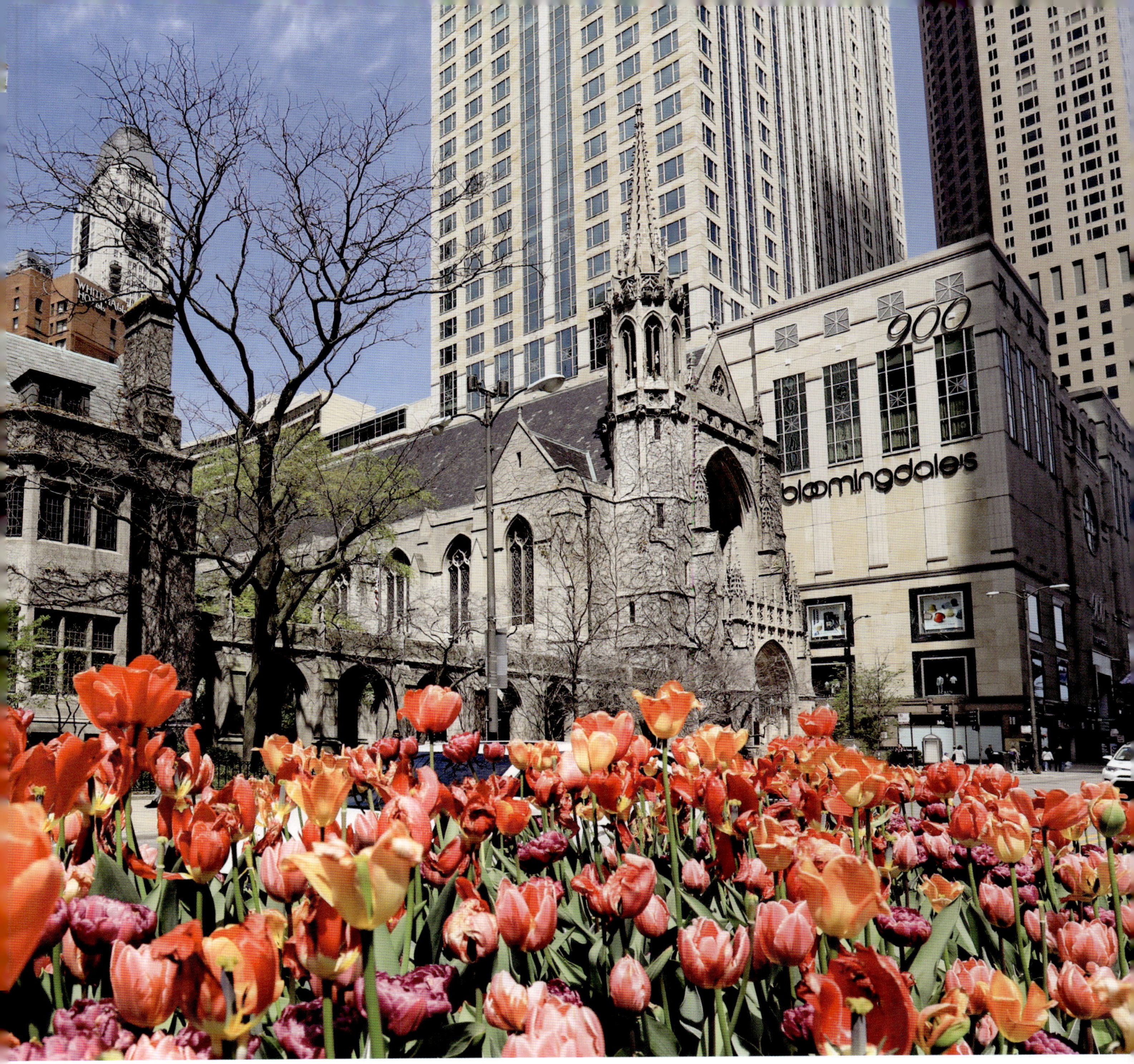
900
bloomingdale's

Temple in the Sky *(top)*

Beneath the First United Methodist Church's steeple is the Sky Chapel. Created in 1952 in memory of Charles Walgreen, founder of the pharmacy chain, this intimate space contains a hand-carved wooden panel of Christ weeping over Chicago, 16 stained-glass windows, and beautiful beams.

First United Methodist Church *(left)*

Located across from Daley Plaza and Picasso's sculpture, this 23-story skyscraper church was completed in 1924. The oldest congregation in Chicago, the church formed in 1831, where services were held in homes and later a log cabin. As it grew, the congregation decided to build this remarkable church building within the city.

Marshall Field Building *(above and right)*

Once Chicago's largest department store, Marshall Field & Company occupied this space until its merger with Macy's in 2006. This neoclassical building was constructed in stages beginning in 1893. Its two Great Clocks are made of more than seven tons of cast bronze and hang from ornamental ironwork.

McCormick Tribune Ice Rink *(top)*

Tucked between The Bean and Michigan Avenue, this public ice-skating rink is open from mid-November through March and has quickly become a Chicago tradition since its completion in 2001. Take advantage of free skating lessons offered one hour before the rink opens on Fridays, Saturdays, and Sundays.

Industry and Agriculture *(bottom)*

Initially atop a ledge over the entrance to the original 1885 Chicago Board of Trade building, two 12-foot-tall allegorical sculptures went missing after the building was demolished in 1929. Recovered in 1978, *Industry* and *Agriculture* now grace the plaza in front of the current Chicago Board of Trade Building.

Chicago Board of Trade *(opposite)*

The Chicago Board of Trade is the oldest futures and options exchange in the United States. Located on the same site as the 1885 Board of Trade Building, this commanding, art deco building was completed in 1930 with setbacks at varying heights, allowing additional light to enter the building.

CHICAGO BOARD OF TRADE

MONEY SMART WEEK
MARCH 30 - APRIL 6, 2019

GET SMART ABOUT YOUR MONEY!

Magnificent Mile Lights Festival *(above)*

The Magnificent Mile Lights Festival kicks off winter and the holiday season with more than a million lights adorning 200 trees along Michigan Avenue. Highlights of the festival include a parade that traditionally features Grand Marshals Mickey and Minnie Mouse, free concerts, kids' activities, and a brilliant fireworks display.

The Rookery Building *(left)*

Designed by Daniel Burnham and John Root and completed in 1888, The Rookery is considered one of their masterpiece buildings. The exterior is constructed of a red granite base, pressed brick facades, terra cotta ornamentation, and turrets, and features incredible architectural detailing. Its massive stone arch hovers over the LaSalle Street entrance.

The Rookery Building Interior
(opposite top and bottom)

When The Rookery was constructed, its interior was designed to deliver as much natural light as possible as electricity was in its infancy. The atrium has undergone several renovations resulting in white marble embellished with gold geometric patterning, chandeliers with prismatic glass, and beautiful staircases.

43

University of Chicago Campus *(top)*

Consistently ranked as one of the top 10 universities in the world, the University of Chicago is a private institution that is known for its rigorous academic programs, offering more than 100 majors and minors. Famous alumni include Kurt Vonnegut, David Rockefeller, and Chicago's first African American Mayor, Lori Lightfoot.

William Rainey Harper Memorial Library *(bottom)*

Inspired by the great libraries of Oxford, Cambridge, and universities in the United States, architects Shepley, Rutan & Coolidge designed the Gothic William Rainey Harper Memorial Library in 1912. Today, it is a study and reading space of the Arley D. Cathey Learning Center.

University of Chicago Campus *(opposite)*

From Gothic to art deco to contemporary, the campus of the University of Chicago is a series of quadrangles that begin at 55th Street and sweep down toward Lake Michigan. Noteworthy buildings such as the Rockefeller Memorial Chapel, The Knapp Center, and the Oriental Institute demonstrate the university's diverse architecture.

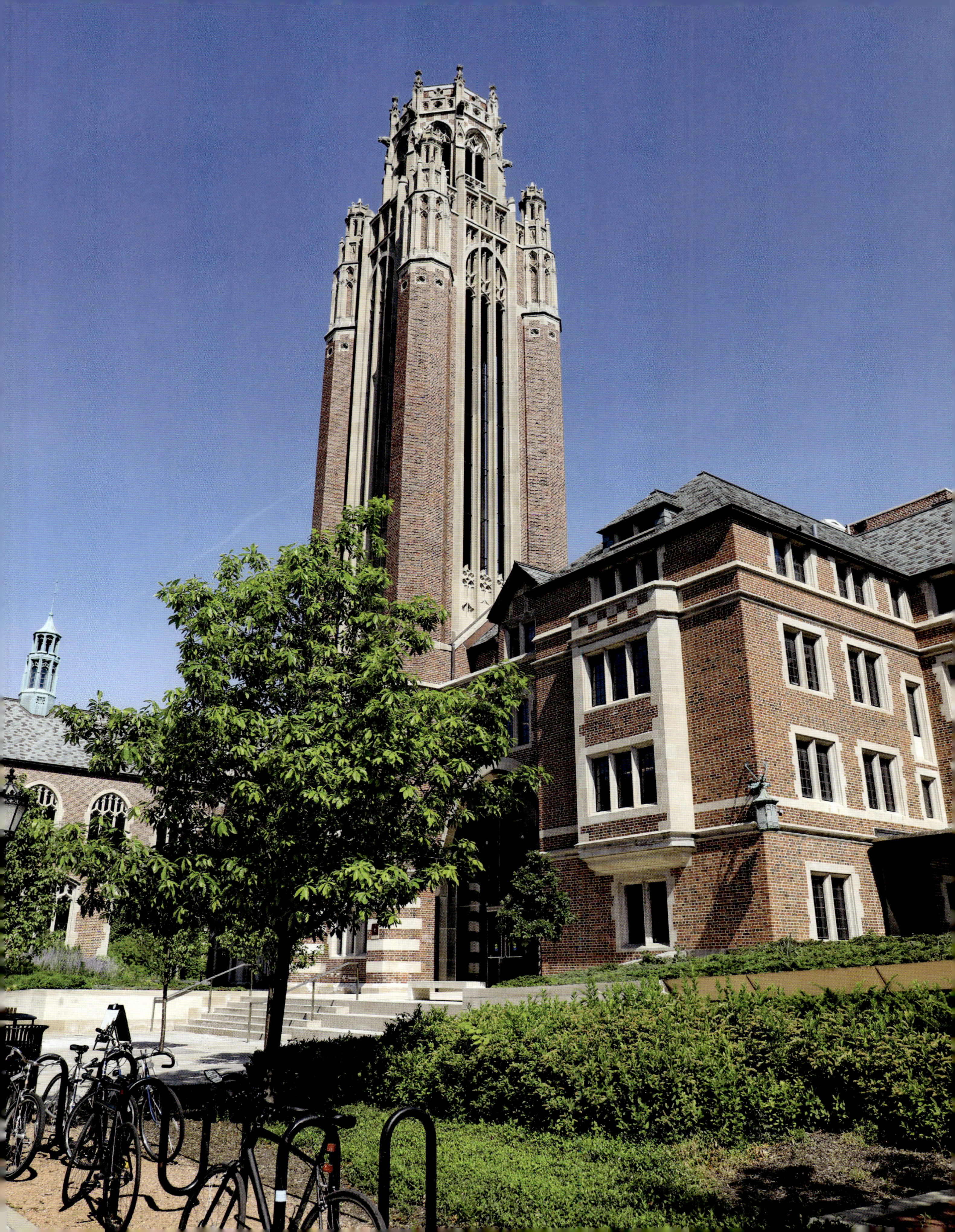

Rockefeller Memorial Chapel *(above)*

The University of Chicago's Rockefeller Memorial Chapel was a gift of John D. Rockefeller. The impressive Gothic building was completed in 1928 and was intended to be the central feature of the university. It is decorated with numerous sculptural works and eight kneeling angels situated above the arched entryway.

Chapel Organ *(left)*

One of four University organs, E.M. Skinner's Opus 634 organ was built at the same time the Rockefeller Memorial Chapel was constructed. Emulating the sounds of a symphony orchestra and choral voices, it has 8,565 pipes in 132 ranks and has undergone meticulous restorations over the years.

Carl von Linné Monument *(above)*

Unveiled in Lincoln Park in 1891, this monument to Swedish biologist Carl von Linné moved to the grounds of the University of Chicago after spending 85 years in the park. It is a replica of a Stockholm monument that originally included four female figures representing zoology, medicine, mineralogy, and botany.

Cobb Lecture Hall *(right)*

Noted for being the first building completed when the University of Chicago held its first class in 1892, today Cobb Lecture Hall is dedicated to the humanities and social sciences. It is home to the Renaissance Society, which presents contemporary art exhibitions, events, and publications.

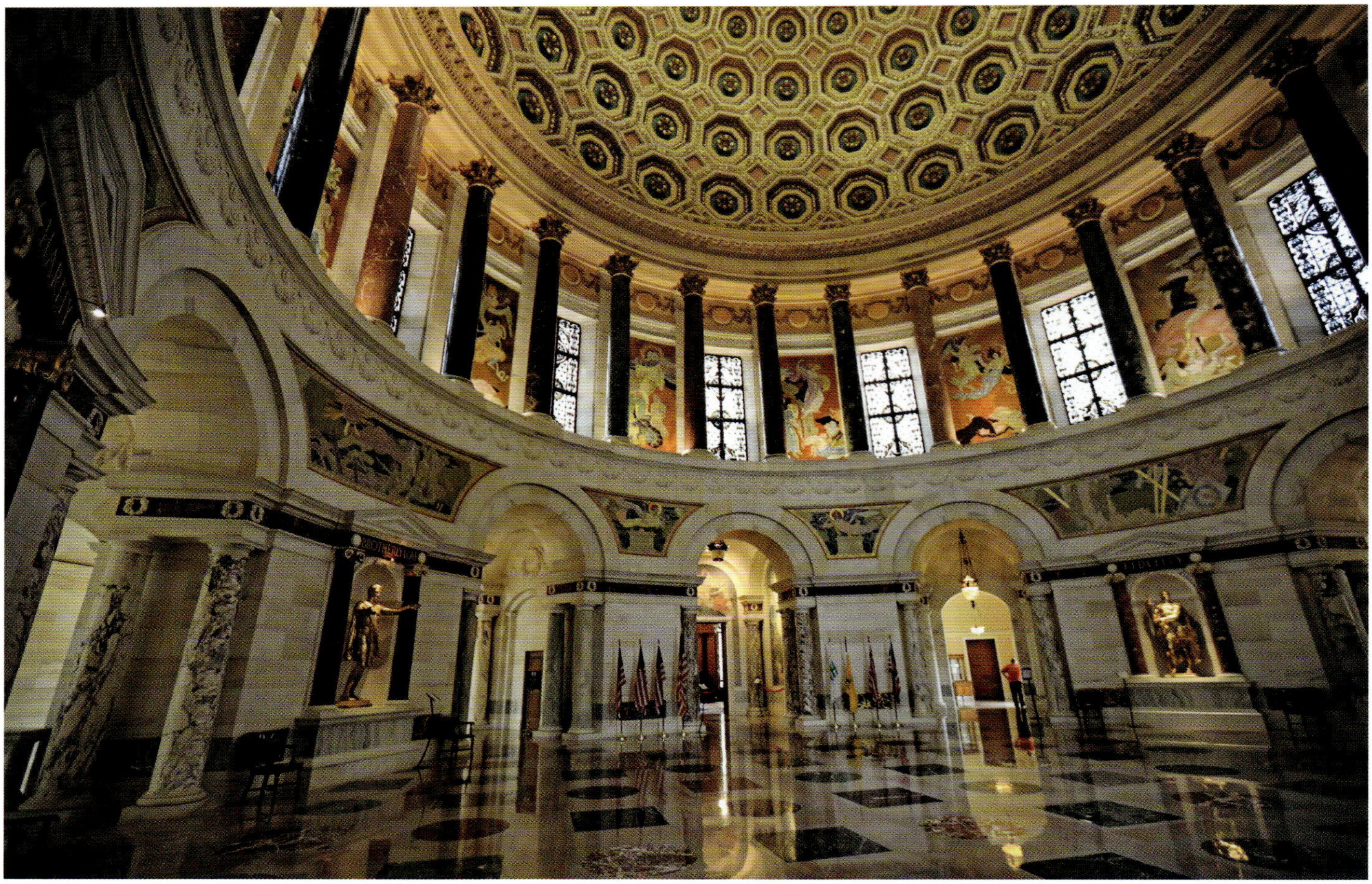

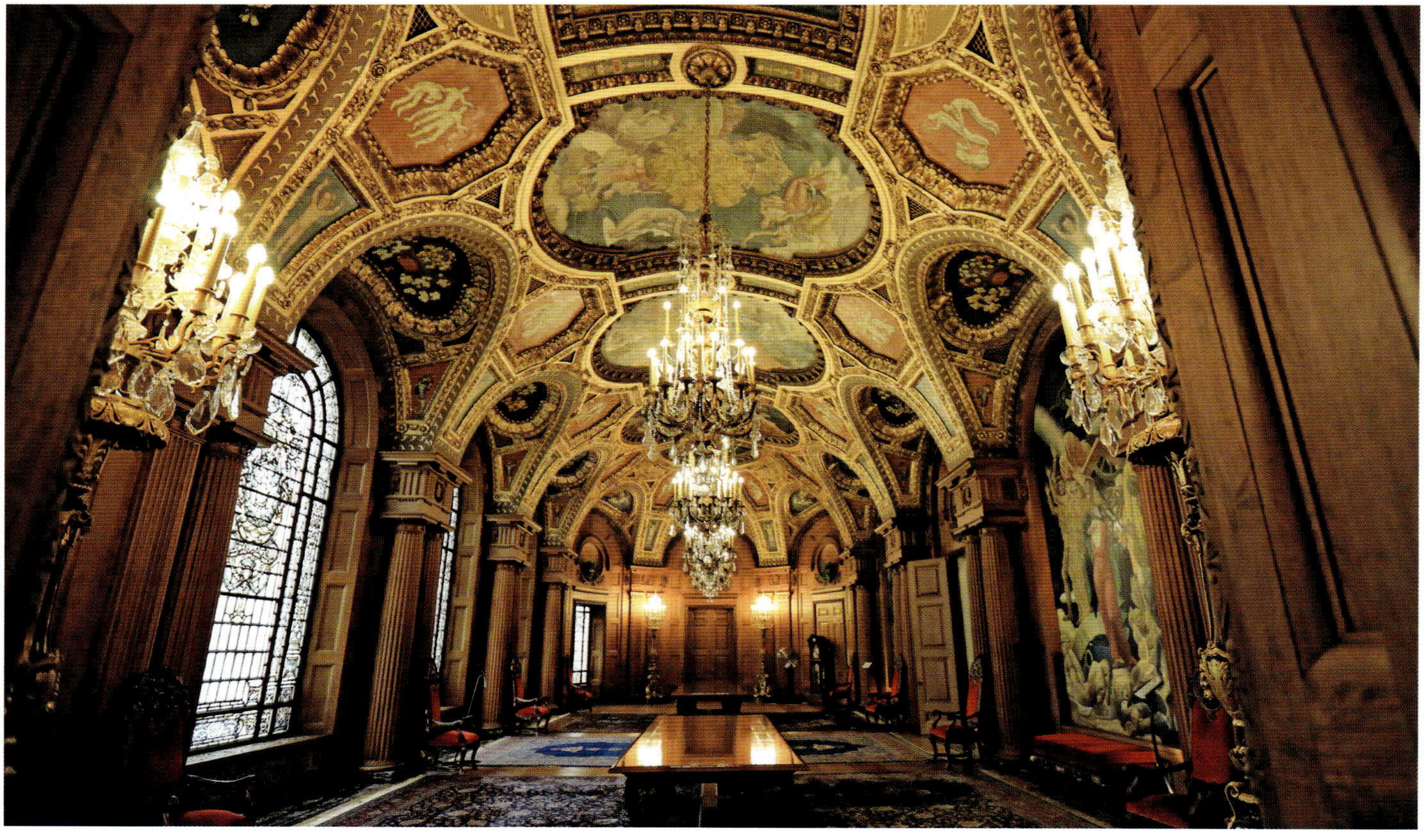

Elks National Veterans Memorial *(opposite top and bottom)*

This magnificent war memorial's columned rotunda features a carved ceiling, murals, hand-painted windows, and statues depicting the Elks' fraternal principles of Charity, Justice, Brotherly Love, and Fidelity. The Grand Reception Hall is a masterpiece of beautiful furnishings and rare woods.

Elks National Memorial and Headquarters *(above)*

Following WWI, the Elks organization erected this distinctive, Beaux-Arts building as a memorial to the bravery, loyalty, and dedication of the more than 1,000 Elks who fought and died for our country. Since then, the memorial has been rededicated to honor veterans of all conflicts.

The Man *(above)*

Illinois has numerous statues of our 16th president, but none are as prominent as *The Man* by artist Augustus Saint-Gaudens. Erected in 1887 in Lincoln Park, this 12-foot-tall sculpture of Abraham Lincoln was modeled after Leonard W. Volk's plaster life mask of Lincoln and photographs taken of him during his presidency.

Head of State *(left)*

One of two sculptures in Chicago by Augustus Saint-Gaudens, *Head of State* depicts a solemn Abraham Lincoln. Cast in 1908 and installed in Grant Park in 1926, Saint-Gaudens spent 12 years creating this sculpture but died before it was placed in its permanent site.

Heald Square Monument *(opposite)*

Located on Wacker Drive, the 1941 Heald Square Monument depicts George Washington shaking hands with Robert Morris and Haym Salomon, two major financiers of the Revolutionary War. Sculpted by Lorado Taft, this was Taft's last work, which was completed by three of his associates after his death.

ROBERT MORRIS · GEORGE WASHINGTON · HAYM SALOMON

THE GOVERNMENT OF THE UNITED STATES
WHICH GIVES TO BIGOTRY NO SANCTION · TO PERSECUTION
NO ASSISTANCE REQUIRES ONLY THAT THEY WHO LIVE UNDER
ITS PROTECTION SHOULD DEMEAN THEMSELVES AS GOOD CITIZENS
IN GIVING IT ON ALL OCCASIONS THEIR EFFECTUAL SUPPORT
PRESIDENT GEORGE WASHINGTON 1790

Clarence Buckingham Memorial Fountain *(above and left)*

The centerpiece of Grant Park, Buckingham Fountain was donated by Kate Buckingham in honor of her brother, Clarence. The Buckinghams were collectors of fine art and donated valuable pieces to the Art Institute of Chicago. Designed by Edward Bennett, it is considered one of the finest ornamental fountains in the United States.

Eli Bates Fountain (above)

Bronze birds, tall reeds, and cattails offset the whimsical, half-boy-half-fish figures squeezing fish in the Eli Bates Fountain in Lincoln Park. Donated in 1887 by businessman Eli Bates, Augustus Saint-Gaudens produced this sculptural fountain. Eli Bates was a wealthy entrepreneur who also donated money for *The Man*.

Kwanusila *(right)*

Replacing a totem pole from the World's Columbian Exposition of 1893, internationally renowned artist Tony Hunt carved *Kwanusila* in 1986. The totem pole depicts the legendary Thunderbird, or *Kwanusila*, with wings outstretched, sitting atop a man riding a whale. Hunt is the descendant of George Hunt, who brought the original pole to the exposition.

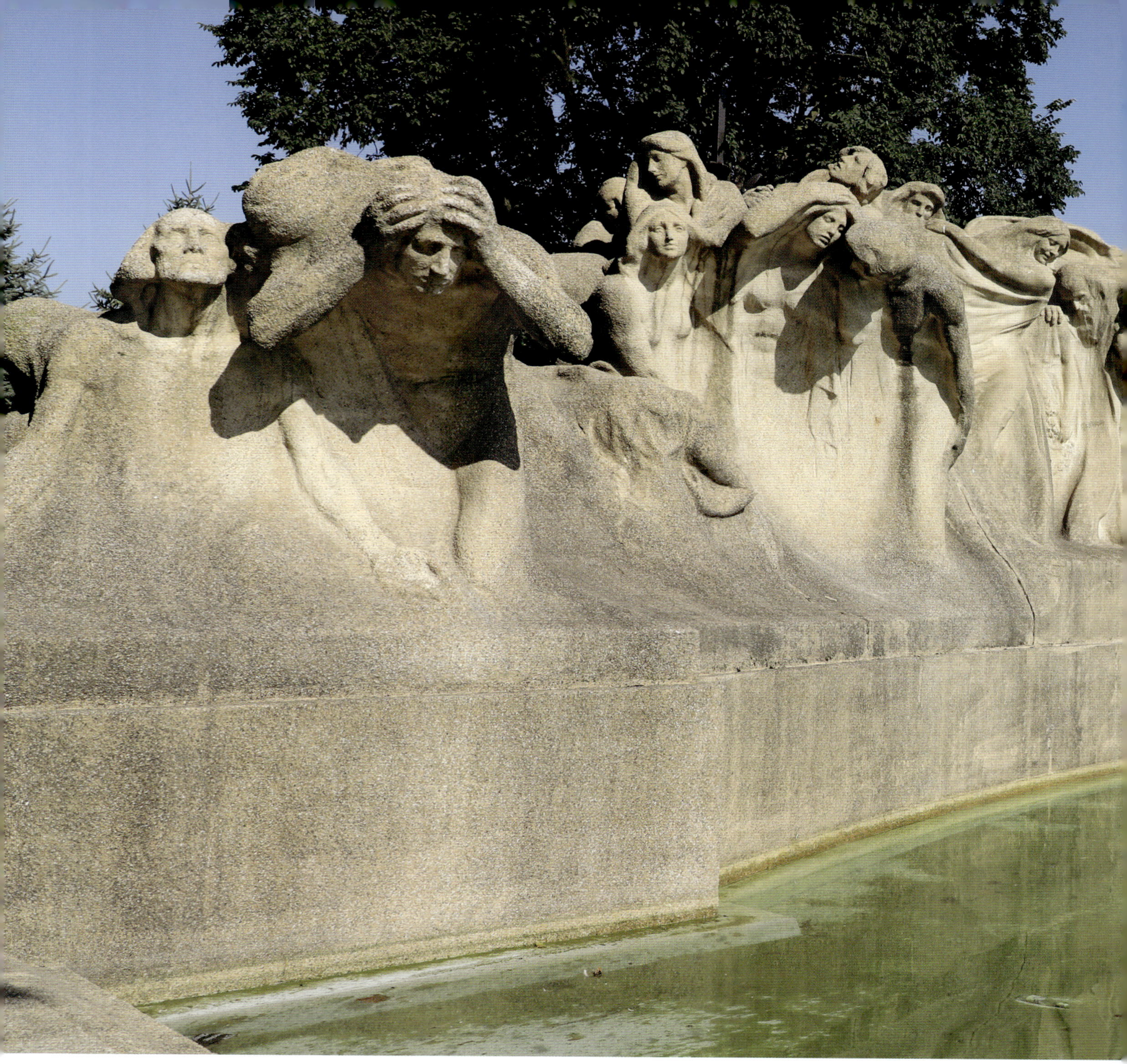

Fountain of Time

A wavelike procession of 100 figures from across the age spectrum is a reminder of how precious our time on Earth is. Lorado Taft's inspiration for the sculpture was from Henry Austin Dobson's poem, *Paradox of Time*. The 126-foot-long sculpture is in Washington Park and was dedicated in 1922.

The Bowman *(above)*

Commemorating Native Americans, internationally acclaimed sculptor Ivan Meštrović created a pair of equestrian Indians in 1928 for the entrance to Grant Park. Focusing on the bold musculature of the *Bowman* (above) and the *Spearman*, Meštrović left the weapons to the imagination.

Great Northern Migration *(left)*

In search of greater freedom and economic opportunity, over six million African Americans moved from the South to northern cities between the 1910s-1970s. Alison Saar's 1994 sculpture *Monument to the Great Northern Migration* honors the exodus with a figure covered in the worn soles of shoes, with a hand raised to greet his new city.

Ulysses S. Grant Monument *(above)*

Commander of the entire Union army, Ulysses S. Grant is honored for his actions in the Civil War in this 18-foot-tall bronze statue by Louis Rebisso. The Ulysses S. Grant Monument is atop an arched base. The bronze equestrian sculpture depicts Grant in full uniform, ready for battle. Dedicated in 1891, it is in Lincoln Park.

Grant Park *(right)*

Named in honor of two-time President and Union army officer Ulysses S. Grant, Grant Park is Chicago's "front yard." The park totals 319 acres and contains numerous linden, oak, elm, and silver maple trees, as well as fountains and gardens. Nearly 10 percent of Chicago is dedicated to parkland.

Agora *(above and left)*

Artist Magdalena Abakanowicz created *Agora* in 2006, a group of aimlessly wandering legs. Designed to be walked through and experienced interactively, each of the 106 figures is 9 feet tall and made of hollow, rusted iron. Located in Grant Park, the sculpture is valued at more than $3 million dollars.

Joseph Rosenberg Fountain *(top)*

Chicago businessman Joseph Rosenberg bequeathed one of the first drinking fountains in Grant Park in 1893 to "provide the thirsty with a drink." Now an ornamental fountain, German artist Franz Machtl created *Hebe*, goddess of youth, atop the miniature classical Greek temple.

Artists and Automobiles *(bottom)*

Installed in Grant Park in 2006 in honor of Allstate Insurance Company's 75th anniversary, *Lilies*, by sculptor Dessa Kirk is made from automobile parts. Five artists were featured in the "Artists and Automobiles" exhibit, which was organized by the Public Art Program and the Chicago Department of Cultural Affairs.

Christopher Columbus Statue *(top)*

Using funds raised by Chicago's Italian American community, Carl Brioschi's bronze sculpture was installed in Grant Park in 1933 as part of Chicago's Century of Progress International Exposition. The Beaux-Arts statue sits upon a pedestal with its four corners representing Faith, Courage, Freedom, and Strength.

Magdalene *(bottom and opposite)*

Located in Grant Park and made from scrapped pieces of Cadillac cars, Dessa Kirk created *Magdalene* in 2005 after the success of three similar sculptures she created as part of the 2004 Art of the Garden installations. Incorporating vegetation into the piece, it celebrates strong women and nature.

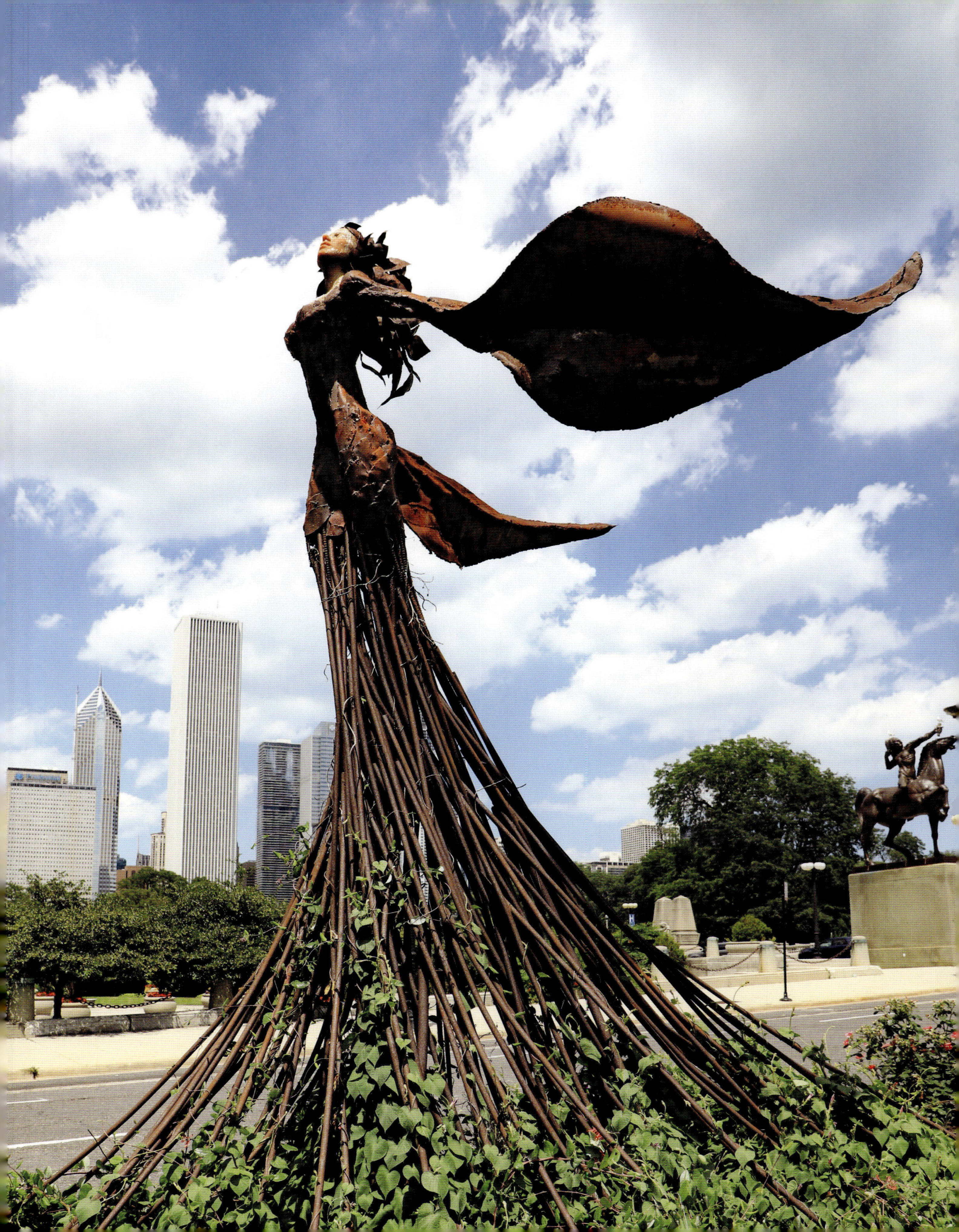

Bloomingdale Trail *(top and bottom)*

A 2.7 mile stretch of what locals call "The 606," a walking/biking trail built on the tracks of a former Bloomingdale Train passenger and freight line, officially opened in 2013. The greenway meanders throughout Logan Square, Humboldt Park, and West Town neighborhoods.

Maggie Daley Park *(opposite top)*

This four-seasons park opened in 2014 and was named after the former first lady of Chicago, who dedicated her life to improving the lives of children. The green space includes two climbing walls with a total surface of 19,000 square feet. The walls are the largest public outdoor climbing structures in the world.

Maggie Daley Park *(opposite bottom left and right)*

Just east of Millennium Park, on the former site of the Richard J. Daley Bicentennial Plaza, the park features 13 intriguing light fixtures and includes a skating ribbon, play garden, miniature golf, an interactive art installation, tennis courts, picnic groves, and the Cancer Survivors' Garden.

63

Chicago Theatre *(top and opposite)*

A Chicago cultural anchor since 1921, music royalty, groundbreaking film festivals, and legendary stand-up comedians have entertained patrons at this State Street landmark. Originally built as a cinema palace, the theatre was granted landmark status in 1983. In 1996, a replica replaced the world-famous marquee.

Art on theMART *(bottom)*

The largest permanent installation of digital art projection in the world, Art on theMart has a 2.5-acre projection surface on the side of the Merchandise Mart. It debuted in 2018, and for two hours a night, ten months a year, the city enjoys its unique displays from the Chicago Riverwalk.

CHASE
CHICAGO
CHICAGO
BRING IT LIVE! JULY 26
ERASURE JULY 27-28
CHASE
LUCINDA WILLIAMS,
STEVE EARLE & THE DUKES,
DWIGHT YOAKAM AUG 16

Chicago Cultural Center *(above)*

Kerry James Marshall's mural on the west side of the Chicago Cultural Center features twenty women representing Chicago's arts and cultural community. Opened in 1897, the center offers free programming, beautiful architecture, unique exhibits, theater performances, and more.

Tiffany Dome *(left)*

Home to the largest Tiffany glass dome in the world, the Cultural Center's dome has a 38-foot diameter and is made of roughly 30,000 glass pieces cut into the shape of fish scales. Located in Preston Bradley Hall, it was made by Tiffany Glass and Decorating Company of New York in 1897.

Richard Driehaus Museum *(above)*

A painstakingly renovated Gilded Age mansion, the museum is located off the Magnificent Mile and explores art, architecture, and design of the 19th century to present. Offering exhibitions, programs, and events, it also features beautifully preserved marble, exotic woods, and Tiffany windows, lamps, vases, and accessories.

DuSable Museum of African American History *(right)*

Located in Washington Park, the DuSable Museum was founded in 1961 to celebrate a once overlooked African American culture. The museum's collection includes more than 15,000 objects that promote the understanding of African Americans throughout history.

Chicago History Museum *(top)*

Housing Chicago's most important collection of documents relating to its history, the museum shares Chicago's stories through films, music, photos, fashion, interactive displays, and more. Opened in 1856 and formerly known as the Chicago Historical Society, the museum offers ever-growing and changing exhibits.

Nine Dragon Wall *(bottom)*

Welcoming visitors to Chinatown, the Nine Dragon Wall is a smaller version of a wall in Beihai Park, Beijing. The mural contains nine large dragons and over 500 smaller ones. The number nine is believed to be the most prestigious number, while the dragon is the soul of all things of creation.

Ping Tom Memorial Park
(top and bottom left)

With dragon pillars at its entrance, this roughly 17-acre riverfront park includes a playground, walking paths, and traditional Chinese architecture. For an alternative gateway to Chinatown, take the water taxi to the boathouse and walk through the Ping Tom Pagoda and natural area.

Chinatown *(bottom right)*

America's second-largest Chinatown is in the South Loop and features colorful architecture, exotic food, tea houses, shops, art exhibitions, museums, and more. The Pui Tak Center, located in the former On Leong Chinese Merchants Association Building, was constructed in 1926 and is Chinatown's only historical landmark.

The Oriental Institute *(top)*

The Oriental Institute has been part of the University of Chicago's research center for ancient Near Eastern Studies since 1919. Founded by Professor James Henry Breasted, the institute continues significant archeological expeditions throughout the Middle East, as well as cultural, historical, and linguistic research.

Precious Artifacts *(bottom left and right)*

With over 5,000 artifacts on display and over 350,000 pieces in their collection, The Oriental Institute celebrates ancient cultures from Persia, Egypt, Nubia, Mesopotamia, Syria, Anatolia, and the ancient site of Megiddo. Included are carved stone slabs, a polished stone bull's head, clay tablets, scrolls, stone inscriptions, and more.

King Tutankhamun *(opposite)*

A prized piece in the Egyptian Gallery is one of a pair of statues excavated in Luxor by the institute in 1930. The colossal statue of King Tutankhamun stands over 16 feet and is the tallest Egyptian sculpture in the Western Hemisphere. Its twin is in Cairo, Egypt.

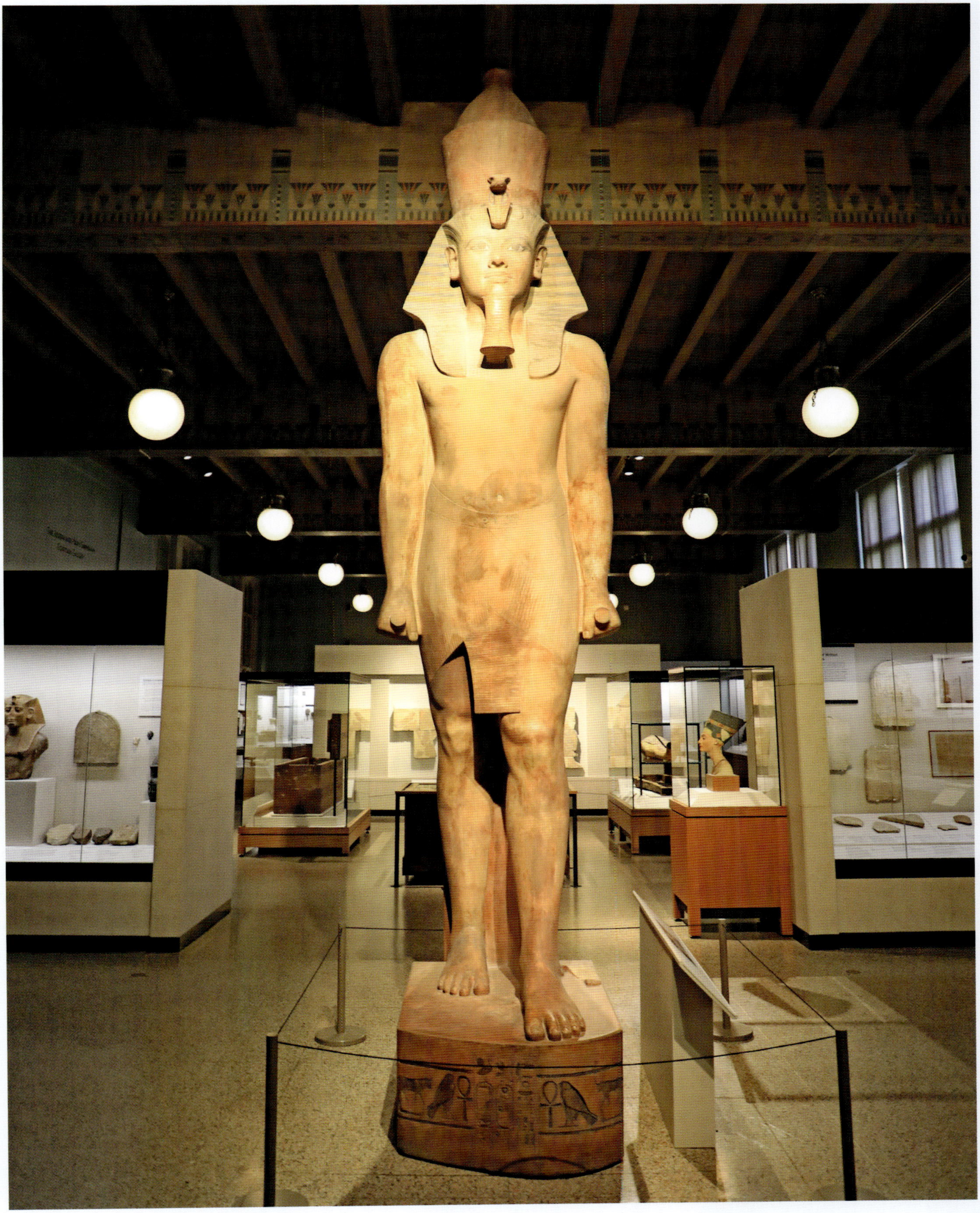

Kenneth C. Griffin Museum of Science and Industry *(top)*

Housed in the former Palace of Fine Arts building from the 1893 World's Columbian Exposition, the museum's building is an alluring juxtaposition to its cutting-edge exhibits in science and technology. With more than 35,000 artifacts, it is the largest science museum in the Western Hemisphere.

Pioneer Zephyr *(bottom)*

In 1934, *Pioneer Zephyr* completed a non-stop, record-setting speed run from Denver to Chicago, at which time it entered regular service with national acclaim. This sleek, art deco train was donated to the museum in 1960. Today, visitors can board the train and see what railroad travel was like during that time.

Man Enters the Cosmos *(top)*

Located on the grounds of Adler Planetarium and overlooking Chicago's skyline, *Man Enters the Cosmos* is a 13-foot-tall equatorial sundial created in 1980 by artist Henry Moore. Commissioned by the B.F. Ferguson Monument Fund, it pays tribute to the space program that was launched in the second half of the 20th century.

Adler Planetarium *(bottom)*

Opened in 1930, the first planetarium in the Western Hemisphere is consistently on the "best of" lists, year after year. Night or day, it has everything space explorers may be interested in, from the largest aperture telescope open to the public to multiple immersive theater sky shows, to hands-on learning, and more.

Children's Garden

Located inside the Children's Garden in Burnham Park, *Culture Earth* and *Earth's Moon* are two climbing features created by landscape architect Peter Lindsay Schaudt. The nautilus-shaped garden was installed in 2002 and is filled with symbolism of the Earth and includes two main garden areas.

Museum Campus *(top)*

Completed in 1998 after the removal of roadways and the creation of picturesque, walkable green space, Museum Campus links the Shedd Aquarium, Adler Planetarium, and the Field Museum of Natural History. This 57-acre park also encompasses Soldier Field and the Lakeside Center of McCormick Place.

Museum Campus *(bottom)*

Paved trails within the Museum Campus lead walkers and bikers toward three major museums, the lakefront, a beach, natural trails, and more. The campus' pedestrian-friendly areas are landscaped with greenery, flora, and monuments, and offer the best views of the city and Lake Michigan.

76

Field Museum of Natural History
(opposite top and bottom)

Renowned for its traditional Egyptian mummies, Native American totem poles, and the Tiffany and Co. gem collection, the Field Museum of Natural History houses more than 40 million artifacts and specimens. The dinosaur exhibit includes Patagotitan mayorum, the largest dinosaur known to date.

Brachiosaurus *(top)*

Located on the west terrace of the museum, this 75-foot-long, 40-foot-tall plastic replica of a Brachiosaurus dinosaur is based on a partial skeleton discovered in Colorado by Elmer S. Riggs in 1900. This deep-chested reptile can be seen from Lake Shore Drive and was placed here in 1999.

Sue *(bottom)*

The largest T. rex ever discovered, Sue stands 13 feet tall and is more than 40 feet long. Discovered in 1990, she is the world's most complete 67-million-year-old T. rex. Located in the *Griffin Halls of Evolving Planet* exhibit, she has taught scientists about the biomechanics, movement, and intellect of dinosaurs.

Shedd Aquarium *(top)*

Gifted to the city in 1930 by John G. Shedd, Shedd Aquarium is considered one of the top aquariums in the country. This neoclassical structure houses 32,000 animals and specializes in reproduction and genetics, health and behavior, and nutrition, as well as animal training with a focus on positive handling procedures.

Abbott Oceanarium *(bottom)*

With stunning views of Lake Michigan, Abbott Oceanarium is home to Shedd Aquarium's mammals. The oceanarium opened in 1991 and models a Pacific Northwest coastal environment. It includes four major species: Pacific white-sided dolphins, sea otters, beluga whales, and Californian sea lions. Aquatic shows take place daily.

Man with Fish *(opposite)*

Stephan Balkenhol's painted sculpture of a man with his arms wrapped around a gigantic fish was installed by the southwest entrance to the aquarium in 2001. This playful, 16-foot-tall sculpture sprays water from the fish's mouth into a reflecting pool that features colorful sea-life imagery.

SAVE
OVER 50%
ON FIVE
TOP CHICAGO
ATTRACTIONS
Shedd
AQUARIUM
CHICAGO
CityPASS
SAVE
OVER 50%
ON FIVE
TOP CHICAGO
ATTRACTIONS
Shedd
AQUARIUM

Fine Arts Building *(top and bottom)*

Declared a landmark in 1978, the Fine Arts Building was constructed for the Studebaker company in 1885. When growth forced the company to expand, it was converted into space for artists, musicians, and literary leaders. Today, it houses dance and recording studios, musical instrument makers, and other arts-related businesses.

Ed Paschke Art Center *(top and bottom)*

As a lifelong Chicagoan, this artist, professor, and mentor of Jeff Koons was dedicated to making art accessible to people from all walks of life. After his untimely passing, Paschke's family and friends keep his mission alive by showcasing his work, providing unique lectures, and featuring up-and-coming artists.

81

Art Institute of Chicago *(top)*

Founded in 1879 as a school and museum, the Art Institute of Chicago has more than 300,000 works of art and artifacts spanning 5,000 years of human creativity. It is best known for its holding of Impressionist and Post-Impressionist works, early 20th-century European paintings and sculptures, contemporary art, and photography.

Bronze Lions *(bottom left)*

"Stands in an attitude of defiance" and "on the prowl" have flanked the entrance to the Art Institute of Chicago and overseen numerous expansions since 1894. Sculpted by Edward Kemeys of bronze with green patina, Mrs. Henry Field gifted them to the institute in memory of her husband.

Modern Wing *(bottom right)*

Architect Renzo Piano created the second-largest art museum in America with the addition of the Modern Wing. It is a light-filled framework to showcase European art since 1945 and 20th- and 21st-century photography, architecture, sculpture, and design. It also incorporates beautiful public spaces that are free of charge.

Stanley McCormick Memorial Court Garden *(above and right)*

Located in Stanley McCormick Memorial Court on the grounds of the Art Institute of Chicago, Fountain of the Great Lakes was sculpted by Lorado Taft in 1913. Five nymphs represent each of the Great Lakes and are arranged so that water flows from their shells in the same way it flows through the lakes.

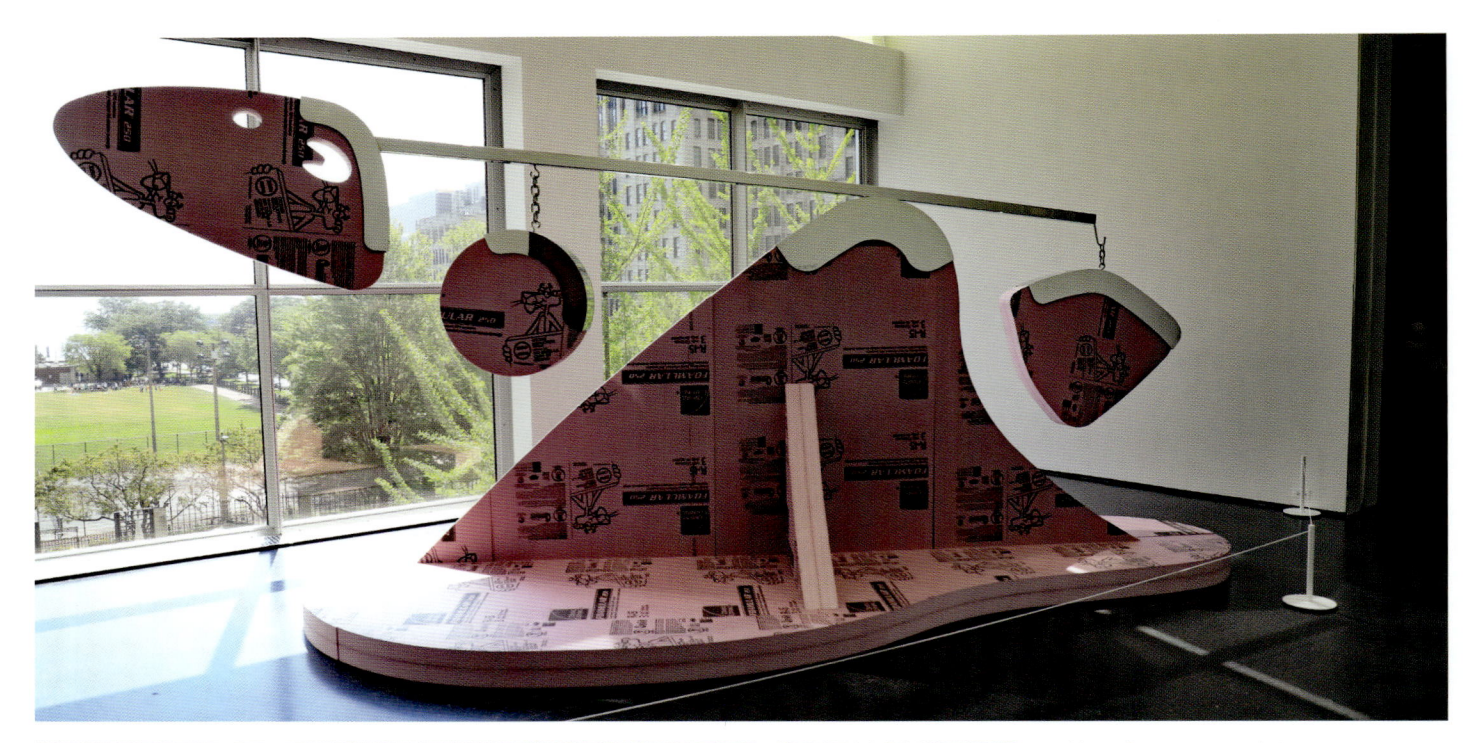

Museum of Contemporary Art
(top, bottom, and left)

Upon its founding in 1967, the Museum of Contemporary Art featured solo shows by Roy Lichtenstein, Robert Rauschenberg, and Andy Warhol during its first decade. Today, it continues to support local art as well as world-renowned contemporary art, performances, and events.

National Museum of Mexican Art
(top, bottom left, and bottom right)

Founded in 1982 by Carlos Tortolero, the museum showcases the beauty of Mexican culture through events, exhibitions, programs, theater, music, and dance. As one of the country's most prominent institutions for Mexican art, it is the only accredited Latino museum in the United States.

National Veterans Art Museum
(top and bottom)

Exhibiting art from veterans of all conflicts, the museum features more than 255 veteran artists and 2,500 pieces of art. Opened in 1981, it is a space for veterans, military personnel, and civilians to address the impact of war. Its permanent installation is based on the book *The Things They Carried*.

American Writers Museum
(top and bottom)

Founded in 2017 by Malcolm O'Hagan to educate, engage, enrich, motivate, and inspire its visitors, the museum is devoted strictly to American writers. Tucked inside the second floor of an office building, it offers interactive exhibits, events, author readings, children's storytimes, and more.

87

Clarke House Museum *(top)*

The Greek Revival style Clarke House Museum was constructed in 1836 and is the oldest house in Chicago. Originally built near Michigan Avenue for Henry B. Clarke and his family, it was relocated twice. Now part of the Prairie Avenue Historic District, it explores family life in pre-Civil War Chicago.

Pullman National Monument *(bottom)*

Constructed by the Pullman Palace Car Company in 1880, America's first planned industrial community was made up of 1,300 homes with running water, gas, and front and back yards. Pullman also had a town square, fire department, school, and store. It was voted the world's most perfect town in 1896.

Hotel Florence *(top)*

The grand, four-story Hotel Florence opened in 1881 as lodging to visiting business people and dignitaries. It was constructed in the Queen Anne style and features a large veranda and elaborate chimneys, dormers, and gables. Saved from demolition in 1975, today it is owned by the Illinois Historic Preservation Agency.

Historic Pullman Mural *(bottom)*

Located on the back of the Pullman Visitor Center, *Visual Interpretations of Pullman* was created in 1996 by students from the American Academy of Art. It depicts a historical view of the town, ironworkers, and the Pullman Palace Car. The visitor center contains exhibits curated by the Historic Pullman Foundation.

Glessner House *(top)*

Located in the Prairie Avenue Historic District and completed in 1887, the Glessner House was designed by architect Henry Hobson Richardson in his namesake style. Rough cut stone and Romanesque arches surround the front and side entrances. Today, it is a museum with interiors restored to their Gilded Age splendor.

Jane Addams Hull-House Museum *(bottom)*

This settlement house was founded in 1889 by Jane Addams and Ellen Gates Starr to aid immigrants of diverse communities to establish themselves in their new country. Addams was the first American woman to win the Nobel Peace Prize and also founded the American Civil Liberties Union.

Union Stockyards Gate *(top)*

This imposing limestone gate is one of the few remaining structures from Chicago's once-thriving livestock and meatpacking industry that earned Chicago the nickname "Hog Butcher of the World." Built in 1875 and commissioned by Superintendent John B. Sherman, a statue of Sherman's prized bull sits at the top of the gate.

National Museum of Puerto Rican Arts and Culture *(bottom)*

Founded in 2000 and located in the historic Humboldt Park Stables, this is the only museum in the States dedicated to Puerto Rican culture and heritage. It houses three galleries and offers art classes, outdoor art festivals, films in the park, and notable performances.

Humboldt Park *(top and bottom)*

Conceived as a beautiful scenic escape, Humboldt Park opened to the public in 1877. Named after naturalist Alexander von Humboldt and covering more than 200 acres, it features a 1907 boathouse designed by world-famous landscape architect Jens Jenson. Swan pedal boats, bicycles, and kayaks are available for rent.

Humboldt Park Field House and Refectory

Added to the park in 1928, the Humboldt Park Field House houses a fitness center, two gymnasiums, meeting rooms, and a banquet room. The park's third historic building, the Humboldt Park Stables, houses the National Museum of Puerto Rican Arts and Culture. Humboldt Park is the gateway to Chicago's Puerto Rican neighborhood.

Frank Lloyd Wright Home and Studio *(above)*

Frank Lloyd Wright lived in this Oak Park home from 1889 to 1909. Here, he and his colleagues developed Prairie architecture. An architectural experiment, the house was designed with an emphasis on nature, craftsmanship, and simplicity. It has been perfectly preserved and documents his life.

Ernest Hemingway Birthplace *(opposite)*

Nobel Prize-winning author Ernest Hemingway was born in 1899 in the first home in Oak Park to have electricity. It is here where he lived and played until he was six years old. The home was authentically restored in 1992, and today the museum focuses on Hemingway's roots and his impact on world literature.

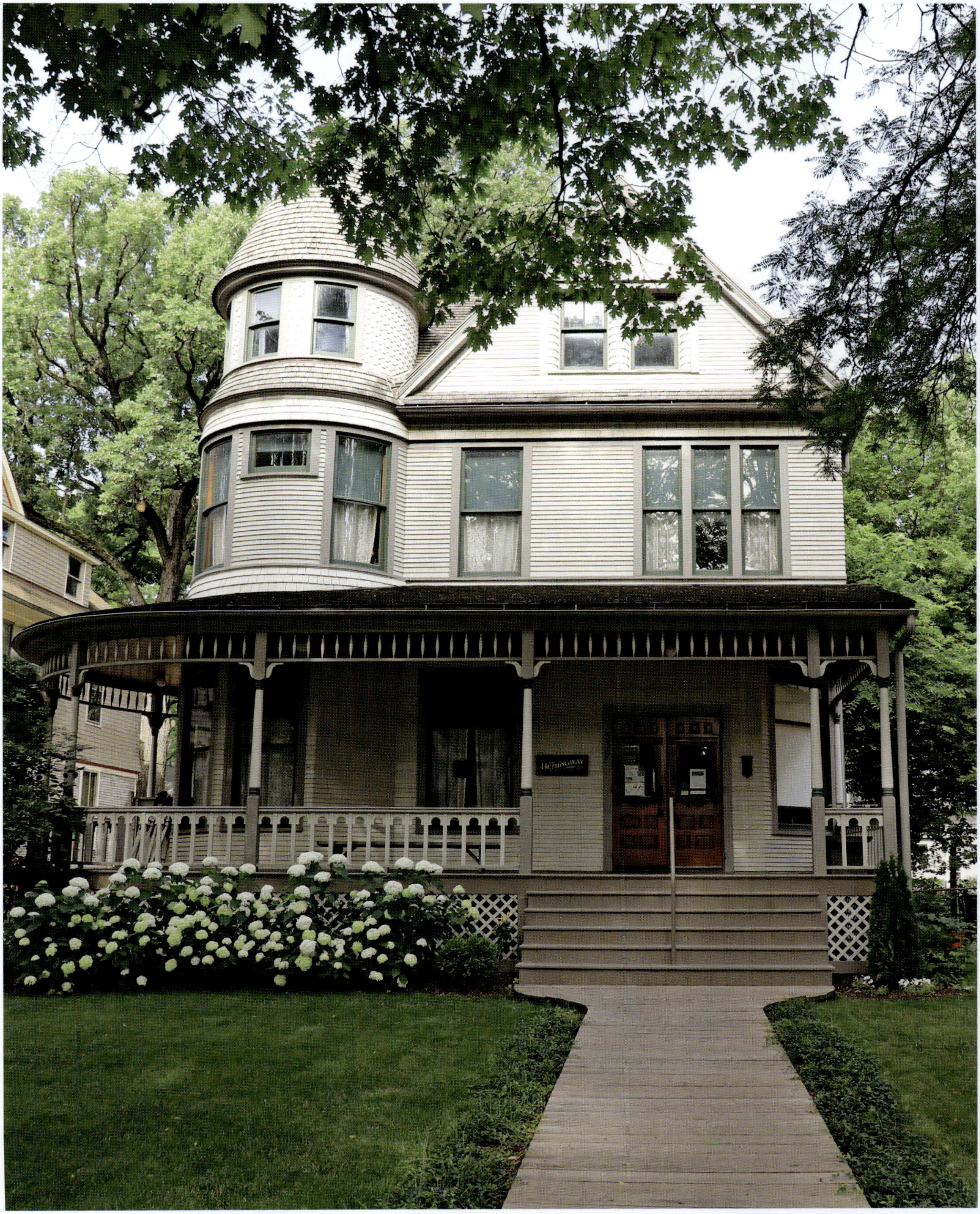
HEMINGWAY

Harold Washington Public Library
(top, bottom, and left)

Named after Chicago's first African American mayor, the Chicago Public Library building was built in 1991. Adorned with owls, the symbol of knowledge, it has over 6 million volumes, an auditorium, and a Winter Garden. It offers original artwork, events, and the award-winning Maker Lab.

Chicago Children's Museum
(above and right)

Located in Navy Pier since 1995, the Children's Museum has expanded numerous times with an array of new exhibits. A place where children are encouraged to create, explore, and discover through play, it has an art studio, play spaces for climbing and sliding, the *Tinkering Lab*, and more.

The L *(top)*

The elevated train system in Chicago has been the lifeblood of the city and the gateway to Chicagoland's neighborhoods since 1892. With more than 140 stations, most landmarks, museums, and popular sights are accessible by one of eight main lines, which are color-coded for easy navigation.

Polk Brothers Fountain and Plaza *(bottom)*

The Polk Brothers Fountain, at the entrance to Navy Pier, is a 12,500-square-foot fountain with more than 150 programmable, arching water jests that mimic waves, schools of fish, and flocks of birds. The pier's front lawn includes a pair of outdoor stages that offer a wide variety of cultural performances.

Navy Pier's Crystal Gardens

Located east of the Magnificent Mile, Navy Pier opened in 1916. Today it is one of Chicago's most popular tourist destinations offering an abundance of sights and activities. Situated within the pier, Crystal Gardens is a one-acre botanical garden featuring a six-story glass atrium, 50-foot arched ceilings, palm trees, and fountains.

Wave Wall *(top)*

Inspired by the Spanish Steps in Rome, the Wave Wall's grand staircase resembles a sweeping wave. Located adjacent to the Centennial Wheel, it offers extensive views of Lake Michigan. Wave Wall Wax, a free weekly summer series, is performed on the Wave Wall performance platform every Saturday.

Summer Fireworks *(bottom)*

Chicago comes alive in the summer. From Memorial Day through Labor Day every Saturday and Wednesday, Navy Pier puts on a spectacular, free fireworks display synchronized to music. It's a dazzling sight that can be viewed from lake cruises, river cruises, and Navy Pier.

Pier Park *(opposite)*

Children and adults enjoy rides on a hand-painted carousel, a soaring swing, and Chicago's iconic Centennial Wheel, which offers a 360-degree view of Chicago and Lake Michigan. Other amusements include miniature golf, a beer garden, IMAX theater, Chicago Shakespeare Theatre, a food court, shops, and more.

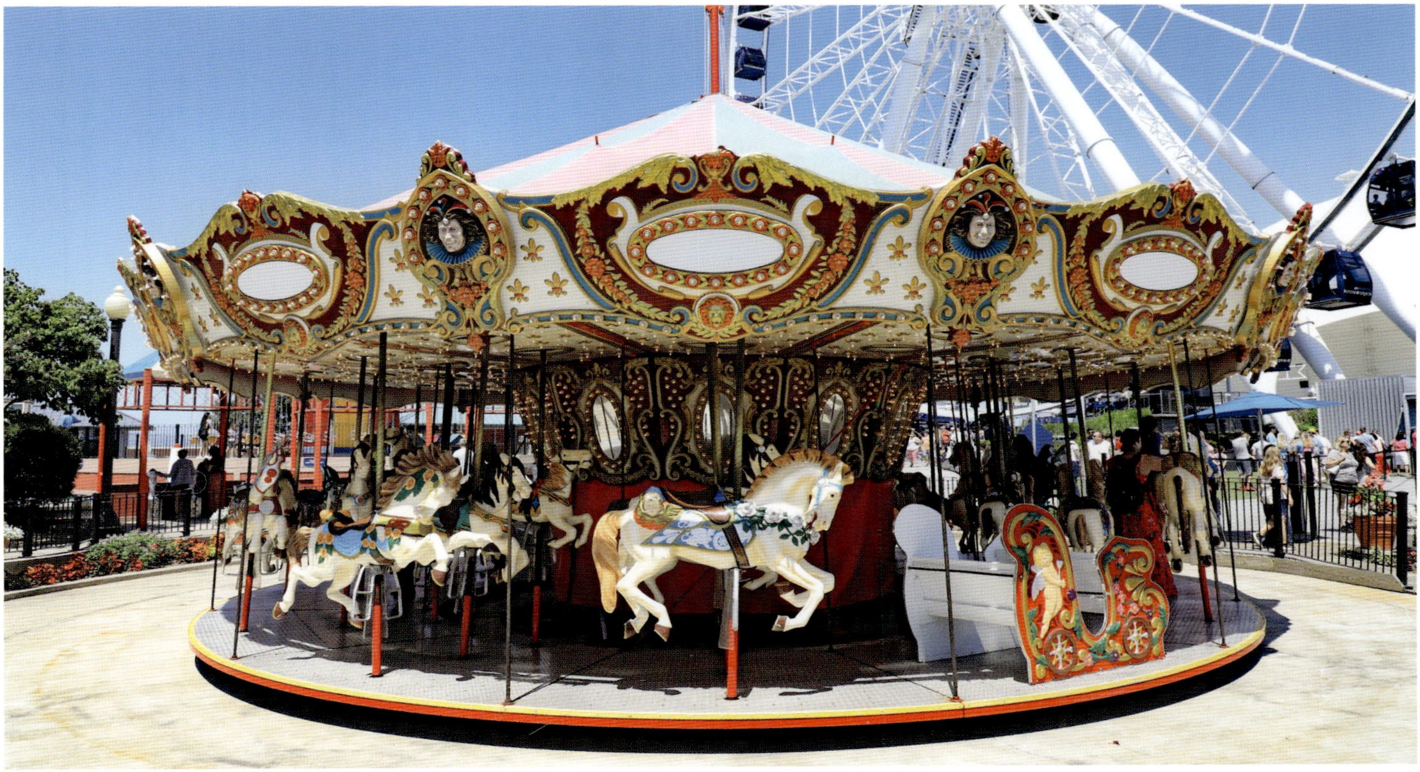

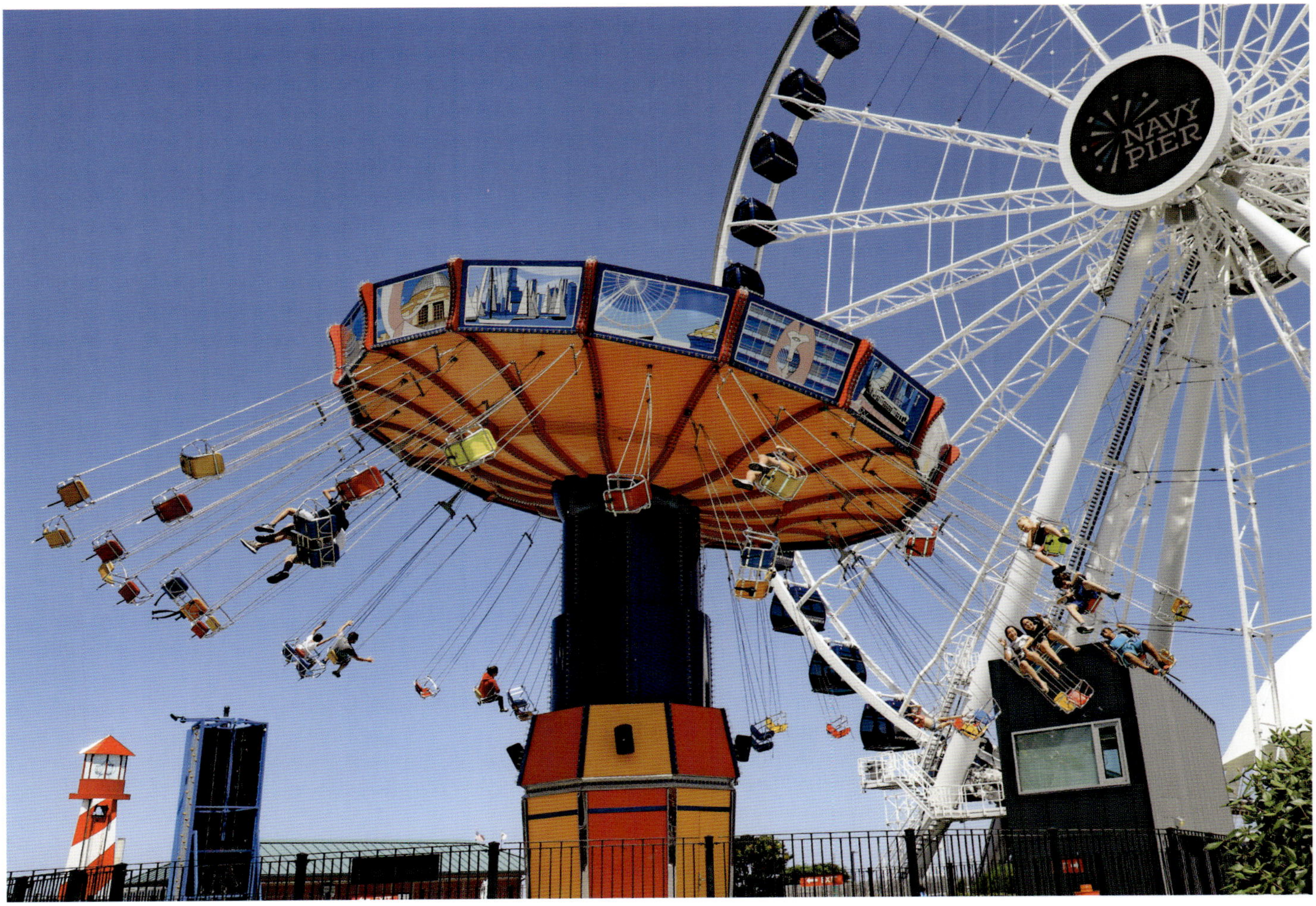
NAVY
PIER

DuSable Harbor *(top)*

Located in the heart of downtown Chicago, DuSable Harbor was opened in 2000 when part of Monroe Harbor was closed-in. Offering 420 slips, striking views of Navy Pier, and easy access to the Museum Campus, it is a great spot to relax and take in the beauty of Chicago.

Monroe Harbor *(bottom)*

Home to the Chicago Yacht Club and Columbia Yacht Club, Monroe Harbor is famous for its iconic views of the city. The largest of the Chicago Harbors and the main recreational water hub of the city, it is in the heart of Chicago and borders Grant Park.

Chicago Yacht Club (top)

Founded in 1875, the Chicago Yacht Club is best known for hosting the Race to Mackinac, which began in 1898 and is the highlight of the Lake Michigan yachting season. The club is situated in two clubhouses and is a leader in challenging, empowering, and teaching children to sail.

Columbia Yacht Club (bottom)

Traditionally housed in or on vessels since 1892, today's Columba Yacht Club is in a retired 372-foot former ice-cutting Canadian ferry. Known for everything from their weekly Beer Can races and top-rated sailing school, to charity regattas and Mardi Gras celebrations, the club's members share a passion for sailing.

Oak Street Beach *(above and opposite bottom)*

Due to storm damage and shoreline erosion in the late 1860's, Chicago's commissioners constructed a breakwater between North Avenue and Oak Street. This created a perfect beach at the north end of Michigan Avenue. Today, sunbathing, swimming, and boating make it the summer see-and-be-seen destination.

Summer Volleyball *(top)*

Summertime beach volleyball has become a popular sport for Chicagoans over the last several decades, with 80-100 volleyball nets set up along North Avenue Beach. With over 26 miles of lakefront beaches, people of all ages enjoy swimming, biking, running, bird watching, fishing, and boating along the shoreline.

Lakefront Trail *(top and bottom)*

Starting at 71st Street to the south and ending at Ardmore Street on the north, Lakefront Trail runs along the lakeshore and goes straight through downtown Chicago. Separated into an 18-mile bike trail and an 18.5-mile pedestrian trail, it accesses parks, museums, and beaches.

Lakefront Trail *(opposite top and bottom)*

During the busy summer months, more than 30,000 people a day enjoy the Lakefront Trail. Commuters, bikers, runners, and walkers take in expansive views of Lake Michigan and Chicago's skyline. Along the trail, there are water fountains, restrooms, and amenities, with water splashing right up onto the trail in some places.

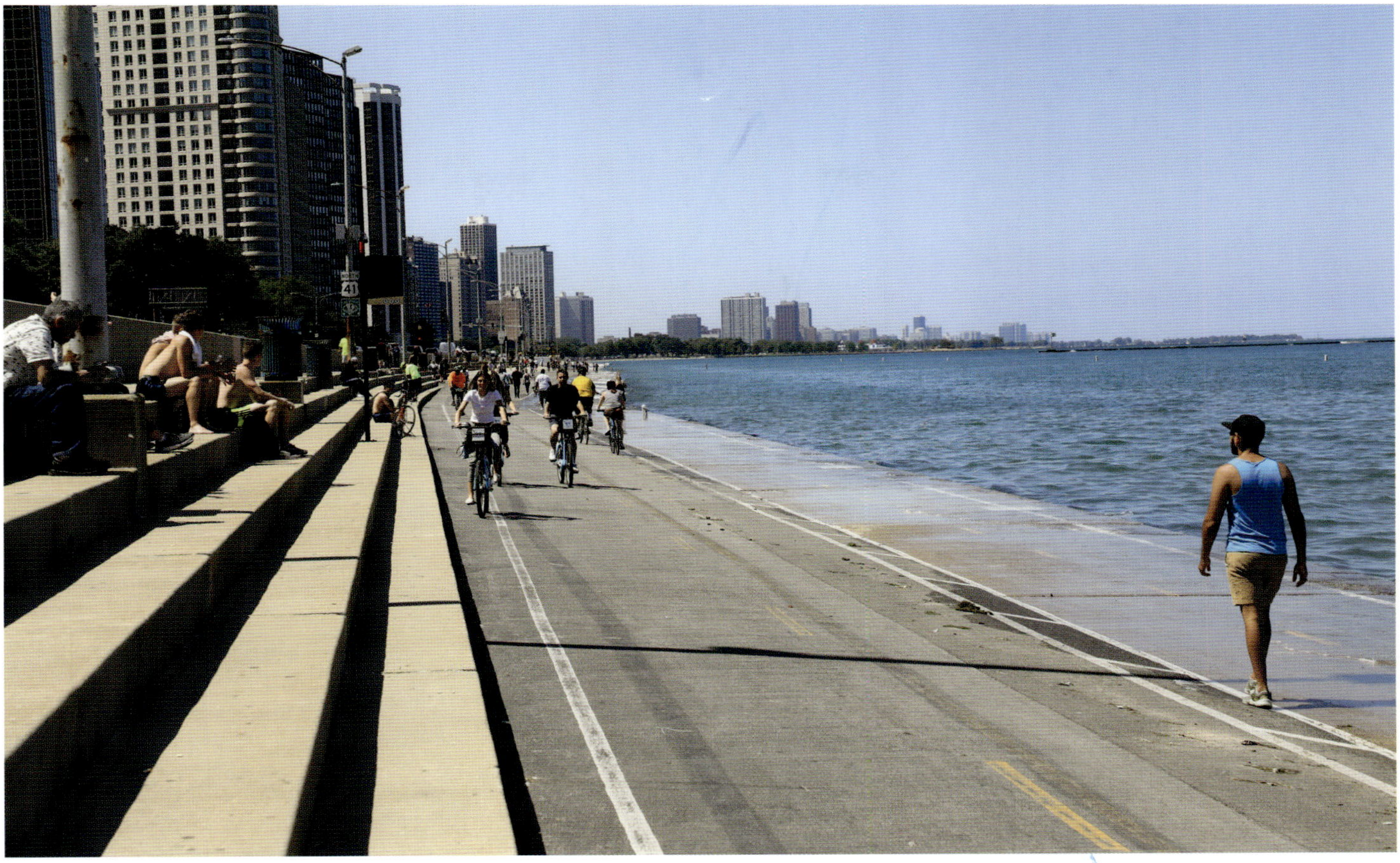

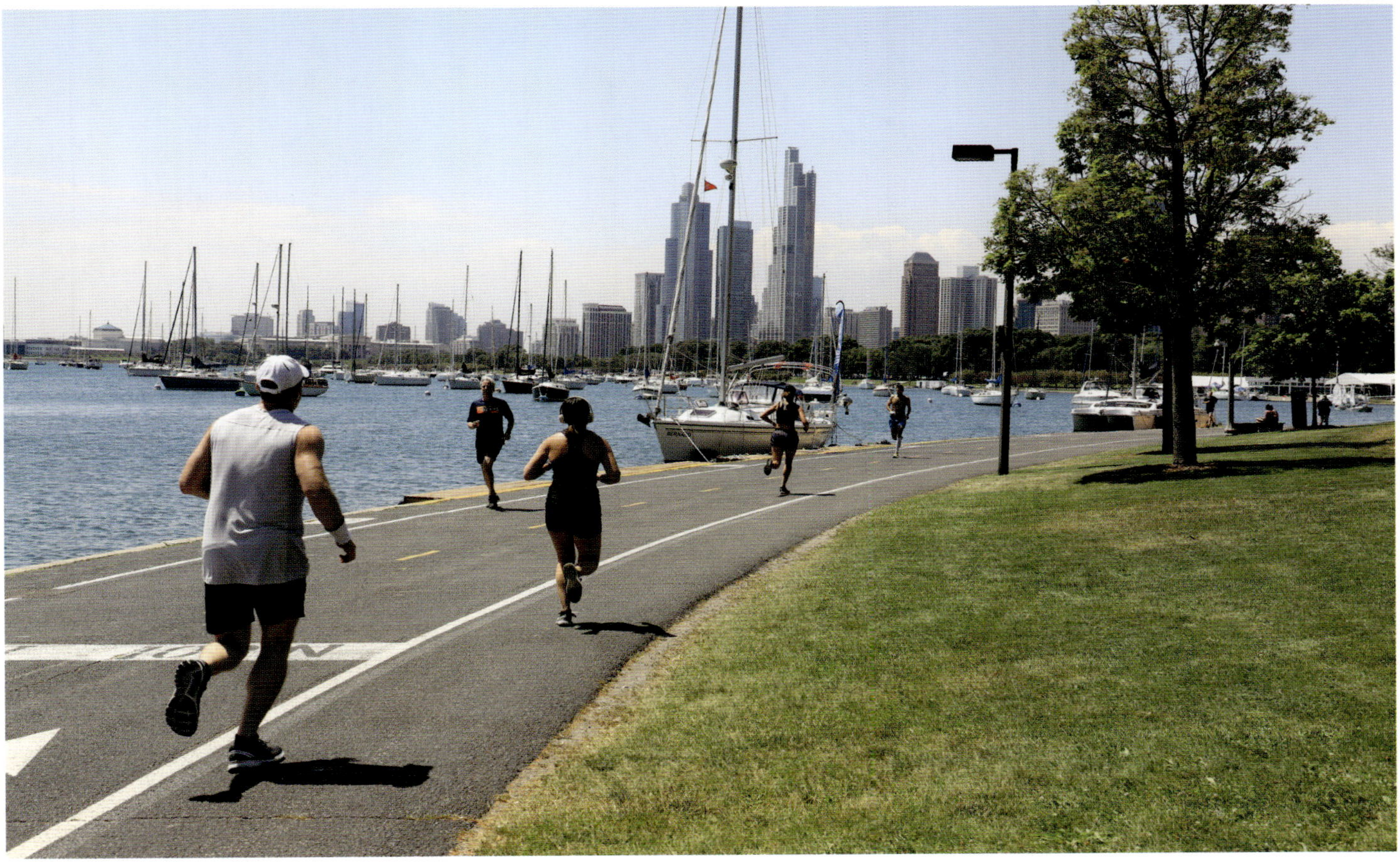

Soldier Field *(top and bottom)*

Opened in 1924 and named as a memorial to American soldiers who died in combat, this lakefront jewel has been home to the Chicago Bears since 1971. In 2003, the distinctive Doric colonnades remained when Soldier Field received an ultra-modern steel and glass renovation.

Eternal Flame of Hope *(opposite)*

Over the years, Soldier Field has hosted boxing matches, political speeches, and was the sight of the first Special Olympics in 1968. In celebration of the 50th Anniversary of inclusion and unity that the games symbolize, the Eternal Flame of Hope monument was installed on Soldier Field's North Lawn.

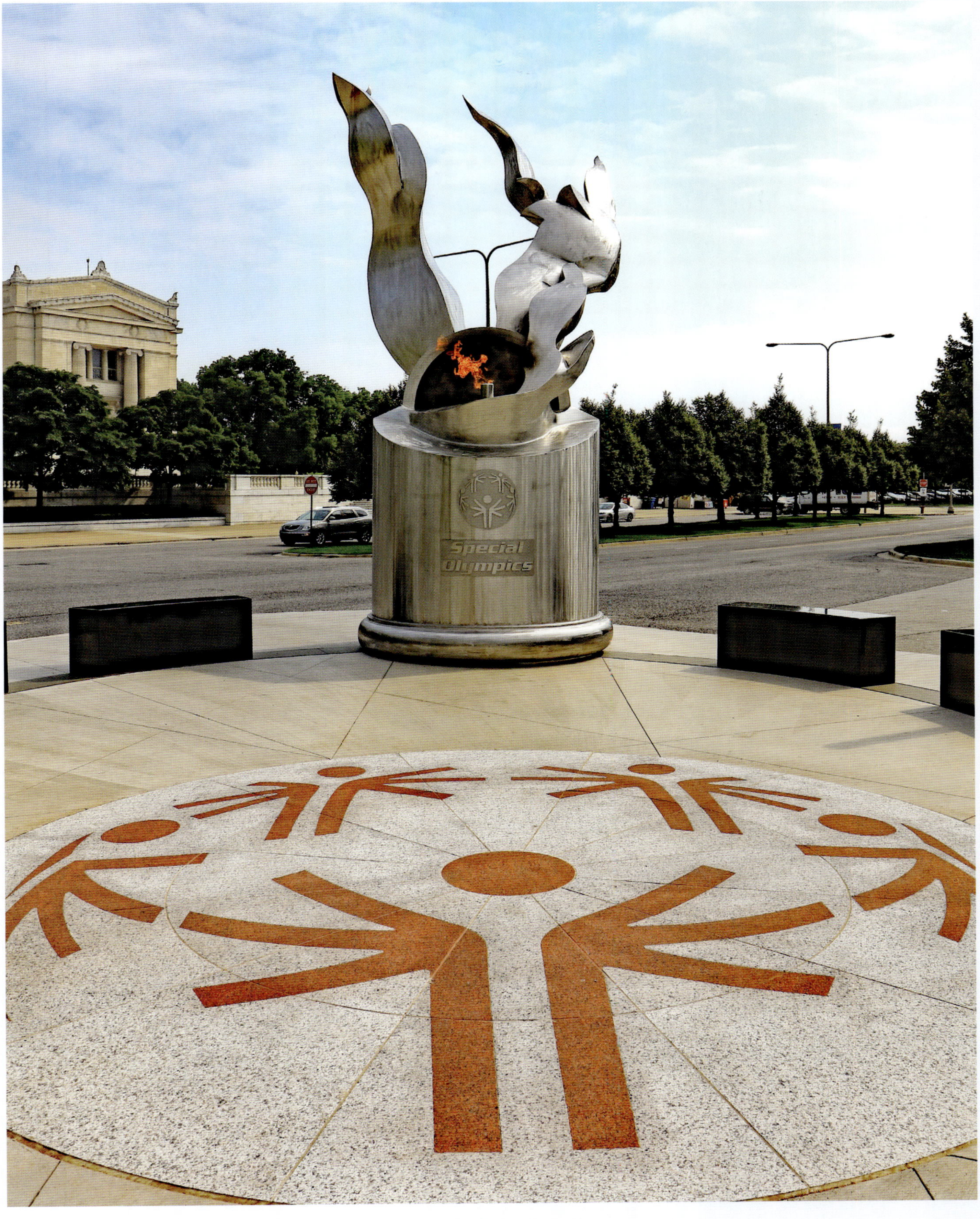
Special
Olympics

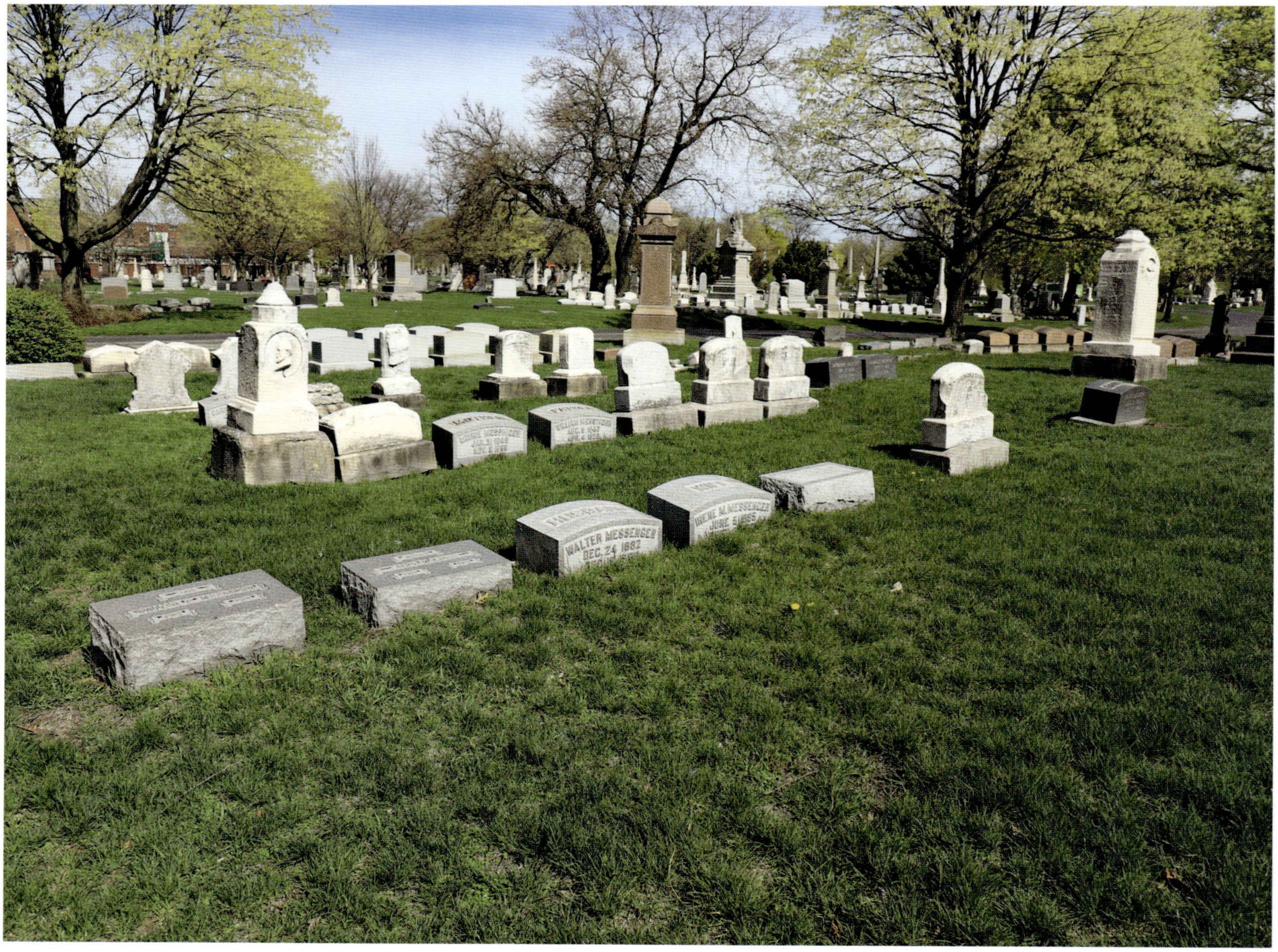
WALTER MESSENGER
DEC. 24 1862
IRENE M. MESSENGER

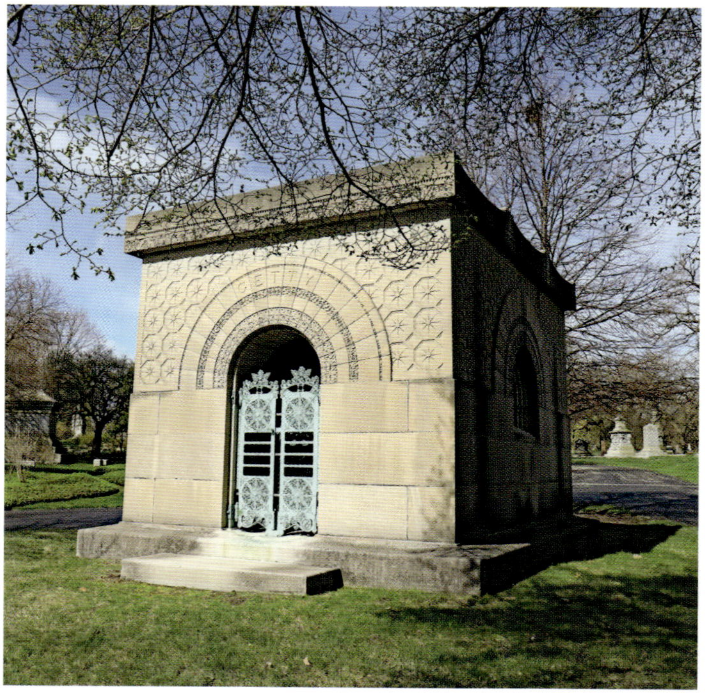

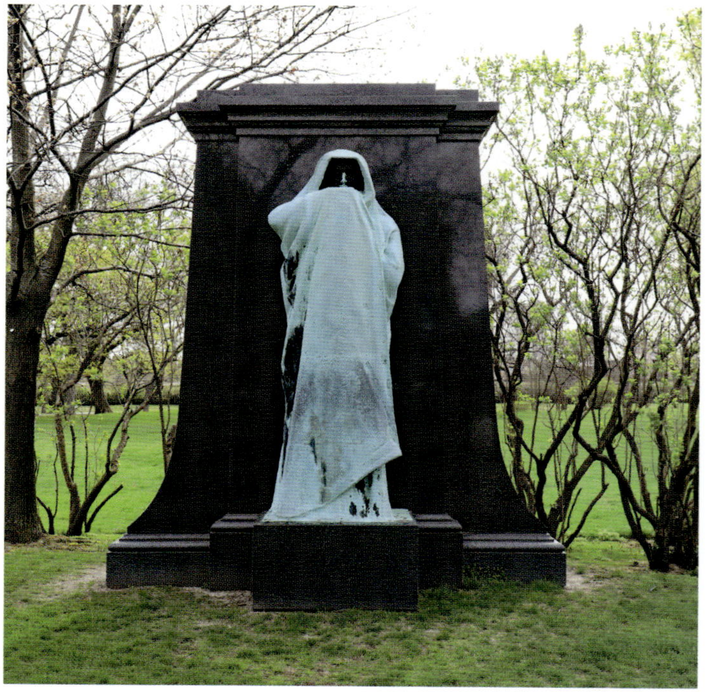

Garden of the Phoenix *(above and right)*

Located in Jackson Park on a small wooded island, Garden of the Phoenix is a remnant of the 1893 World's Columbian Exposition. A gift from Japan as a symbol of mutual respect, the garden features a moon bridge, Shinto gate, Japanese horticulture, and sculpture by Yoko Ono.

Graceland Cemetery *(opposite top and bottom)*

Graceland Cemetery, established in 1860 as a private cemetery, is an approximately 120-acre parklike cemetery and final resting place of many of Chicago's celebrated figures, including athletes, politicians, and prominent architects. Featuring art, architecture, and historic landscaping, it is now owned and operated by the Trustees of the Graceland Cemetery Improvement Fund.

Peggy Notebaert Nature Museum
(above and left)

Since 1857, the Chicago Academy of Sciences has been a leader in nature as well as science research, education, and conservation. In 1999, the academy built a new state-of-the-art facility for its museum, the Peggy Notebaert Nature Museum. Today, it receives nearly 300,000 visitors a year.

Judy Istock Butterfly Haven
(opposite top and bottom)

The *Judy Istock Butterfly Haven* at the Peggy Notebaert Nature Museum has over 1,000 free-flying butterflies of more than 40 different species in its 2,700- square-foot tropical greenhouse. Newly emerged butterflies take flight for the first time every day at the daily First Flight Butterfly event.

113

Garfield Park Gold Dome Field House
(above and opposite top)

Located in Garfield Park, this Spanish Baroque Revival style fieldhouse was built in 1928 and houses a ballroom, auditorium, a boxing center, meeting rooms, and a dance studio. Garfield Park opened in 1874, and today it features a bandshell, sculptures, sports fields and courts, and more.

Garfield Park Conservatory *(opposite bottom)*

Showcasing "landscape art under glass," the Garfield Park Conservatory was designed by Jen Jensen and opened in 1908. One of the largest greenhouse conservatories in the country, it features themed rooms with exotic plants. Designed as a tropical landscape, the Palm House is one of the conservatoire's most popular rooms.

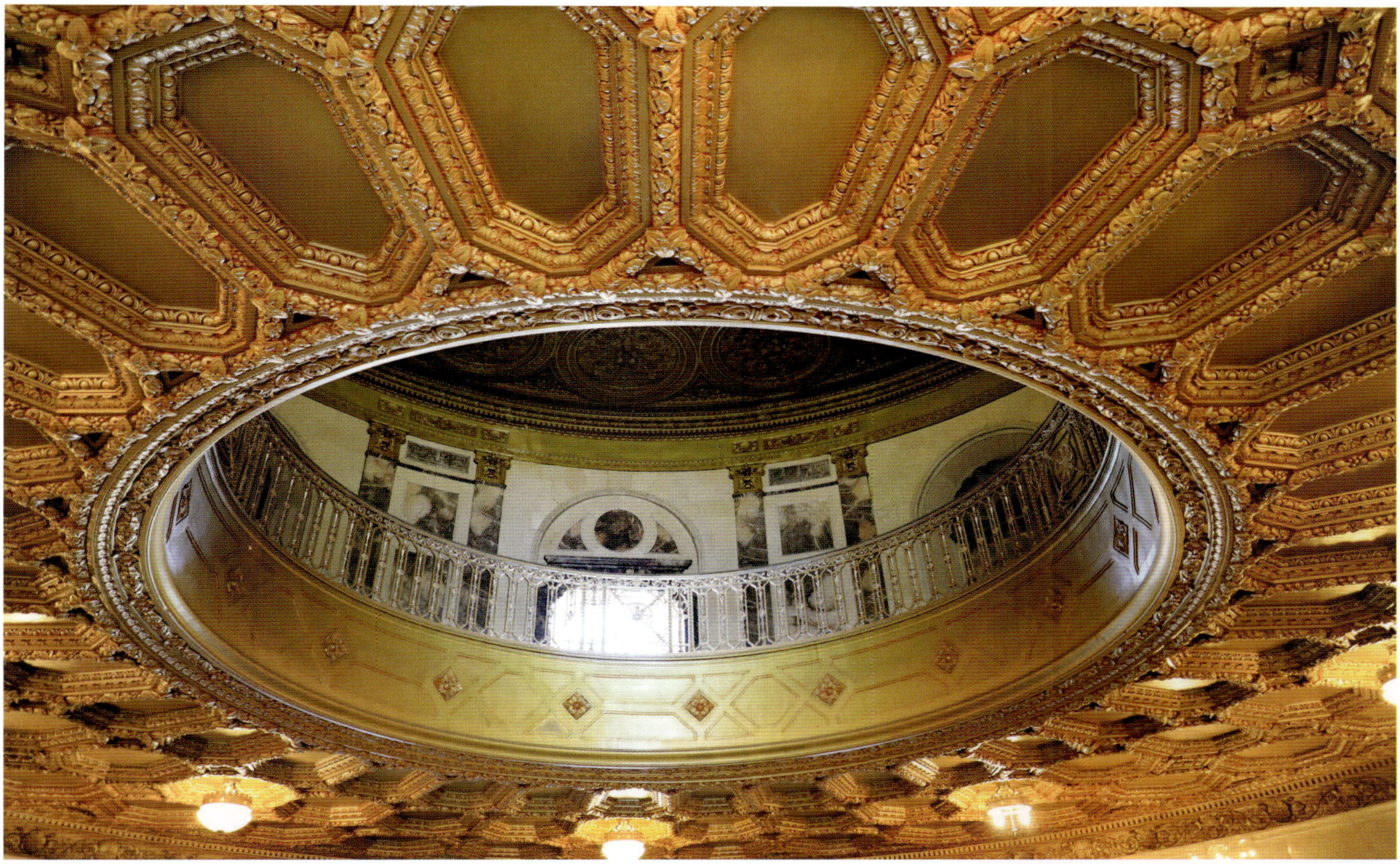

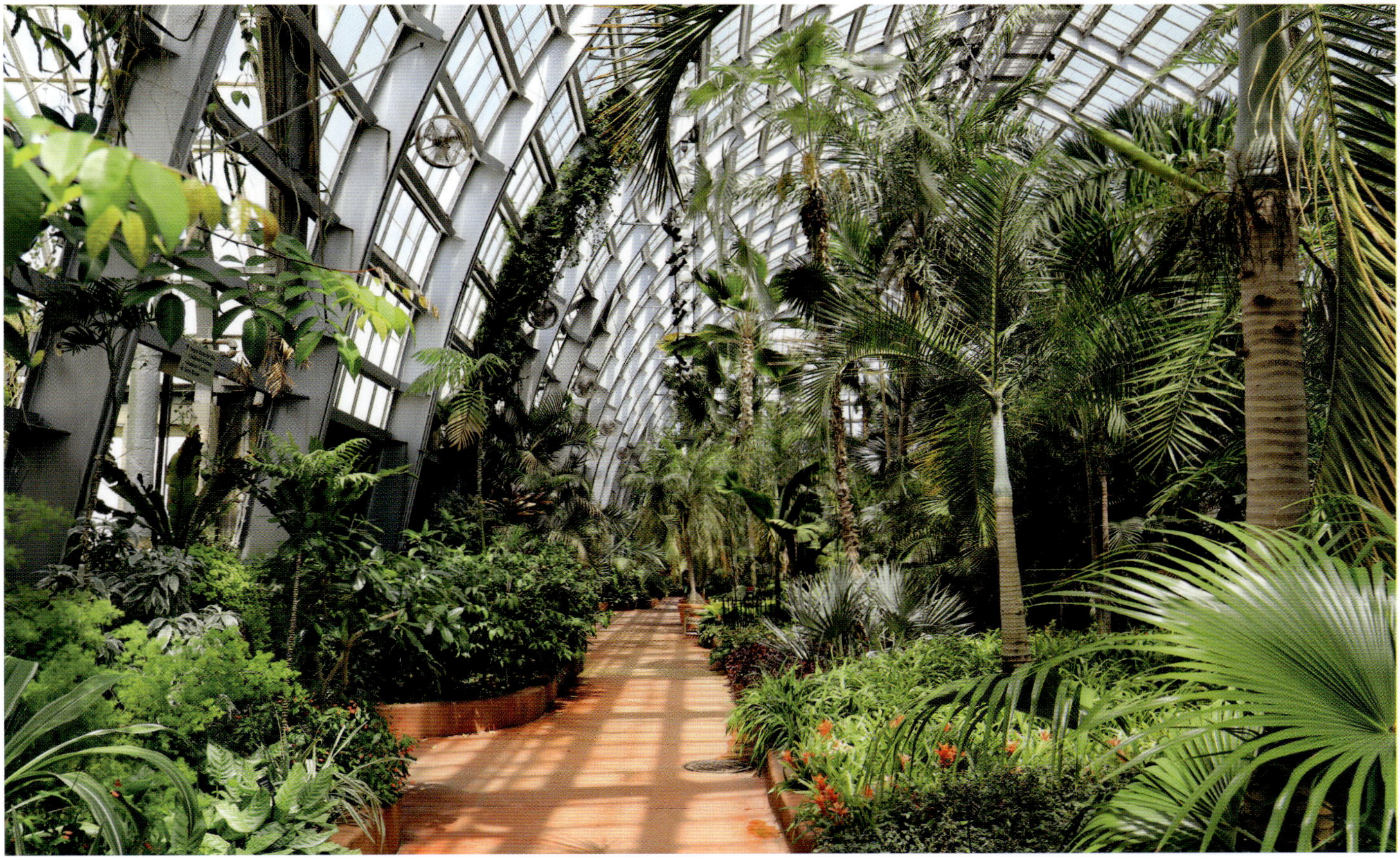

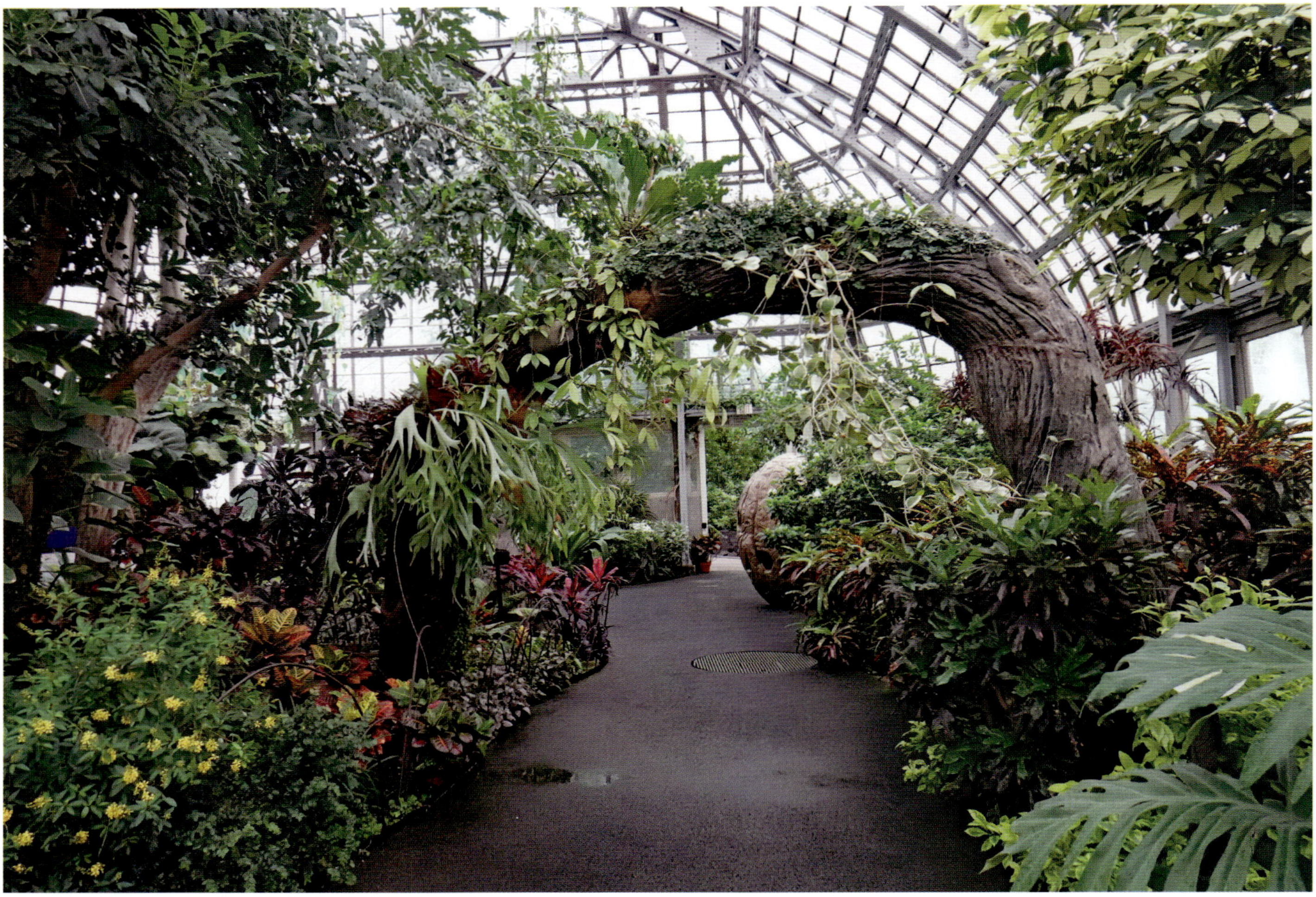

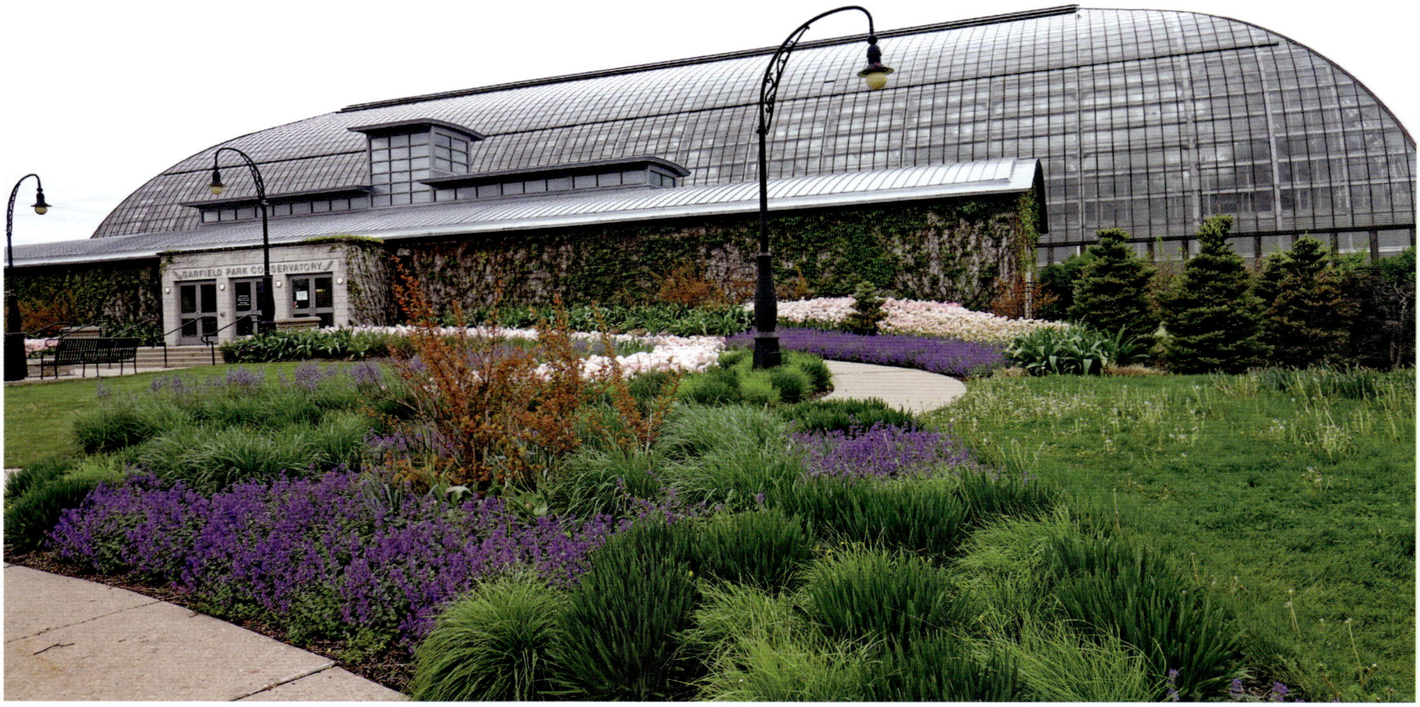
GARFIELD PARK CO

Lincoln Park Conservatory
(above and right)

Located in Lincoln Park, the Victorian conservatory was designed by Joseph Lyman Silsbee and M.E. Bell and completed in 1895. A formal garden at the entrance was planted in the late 1870s. The "paradise under glass" features the sculpture *Garden Figure* by Frederick C. Hibbard.

Garfield Park Conservatory
(opposite top and bottom)

Designed to resemble a large Midwestern haystack, the conservatory's stunning, glass building occupies approximately two acres. Outside are 12 acres of gardens, play spaces, a water lily pond, beehives, a labyrinth, and more. The conservatory also offers programs and events and is an ideal wedding location.

Lincoln Park *(top and bottom)*

The Education Pavilion, along the nature boardwalk at Lincoln Park Zoo, was inspired by a tortoise's shell. Designed by Studio Gang Architects, it provides shelter for open-air classrooms. Lincoln Park offers views of Chicago's skyline and features the Eli Bates Fountain and Johann Christoph Friedrich von Schiller Monument.

Dream Lady Statue *(opposite)*

Best known for his children's poetry, *Dream Lady* was erected in memory of Eugene Field. Located in the Lincoln Park Zoo and sculpted by Edward Francis McCartan, a fairylike figure leans over two sleeping children while holding poppies in one hand. The scene is from Field's poem *Rock-a-By Lady*.

AND NOD ONE
IN A WOODEN SHOE
RIVER OF CRYSTAL
OF DEW
HAVE YOU EVER HEARD OF THE SUGAR
TIS A MARVEL OF GREAT
IT BLOOMS ON THE SHORE OF THE
IN THE GARDEN OF SHUT

Lincoln Park Zoo *(top, bottom, and left)*

The Lincoln Park Zoo is the fourth oldest zoo in the country. It combines conservation and learning with science and animal research to ensure many endangered species around the world will be roaming the earth for future generations. The AT&T Endangered Species Carousel welcomes visitors near the zoo's east gate entrance.

Lincoln Park Zoo *(above and right)*

Connecting people with nature since 1868, children and adults enjoy the zoo's animals from around the world. Among its exhibits is the Regenstein African Journey, where visitors get up close to lions and rhinoceroses. Other attractions include the Pritzker Family Children's Zoo, Kovler Seal Pool, Farm-in-the-Zoo, and more.

Gallagher Way *(top)*

A public plaza and Wrigley Field's Western Gate, Gallagher Way opened at the beginning of the 2017 baseball season. Aside from game day events, it offers shops and eateries, movie nights, fitness classes, free concerts, a French market, food trucks, family events, and a large open space to play catch.

Wrigley Field *(bottom and opposite)*

The oldest baseball park in the National League, Wrigley Field opened as Weeghman Park in 1914 with just 14,000 seats. In 1926, William Wrigley purchased the stadium. Since then, it has undergone multiple renovations, and today there is very little of the original building in place.

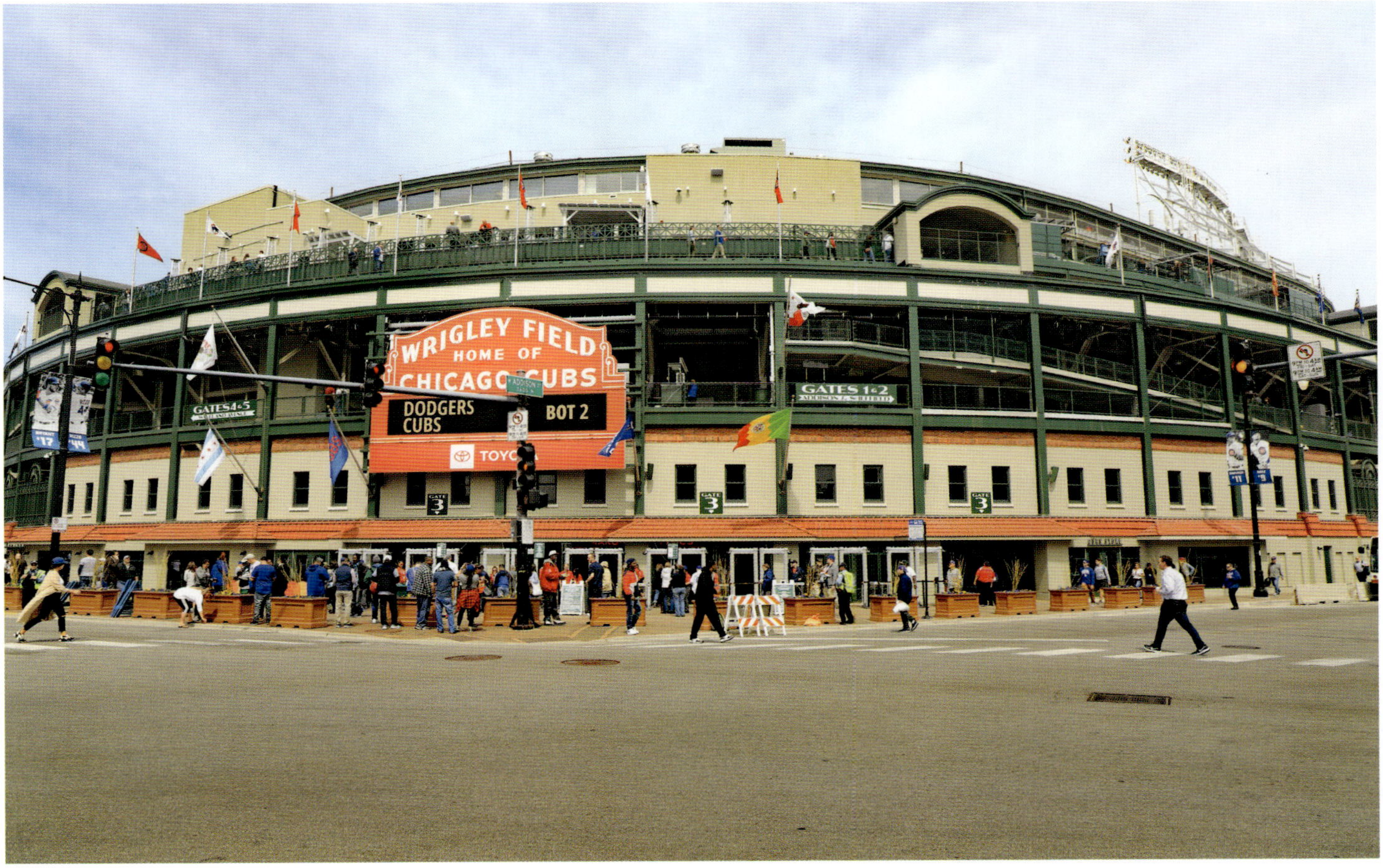

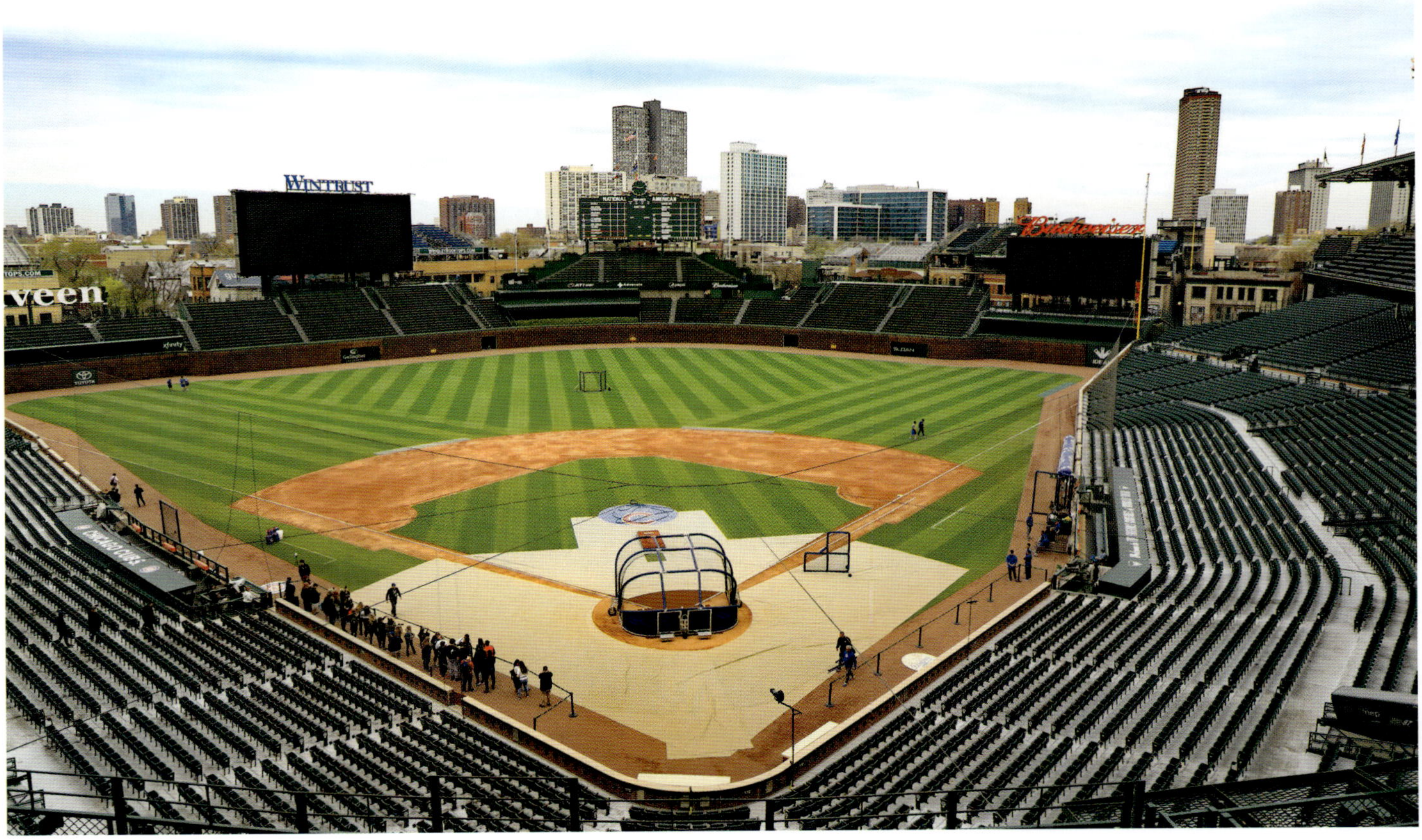

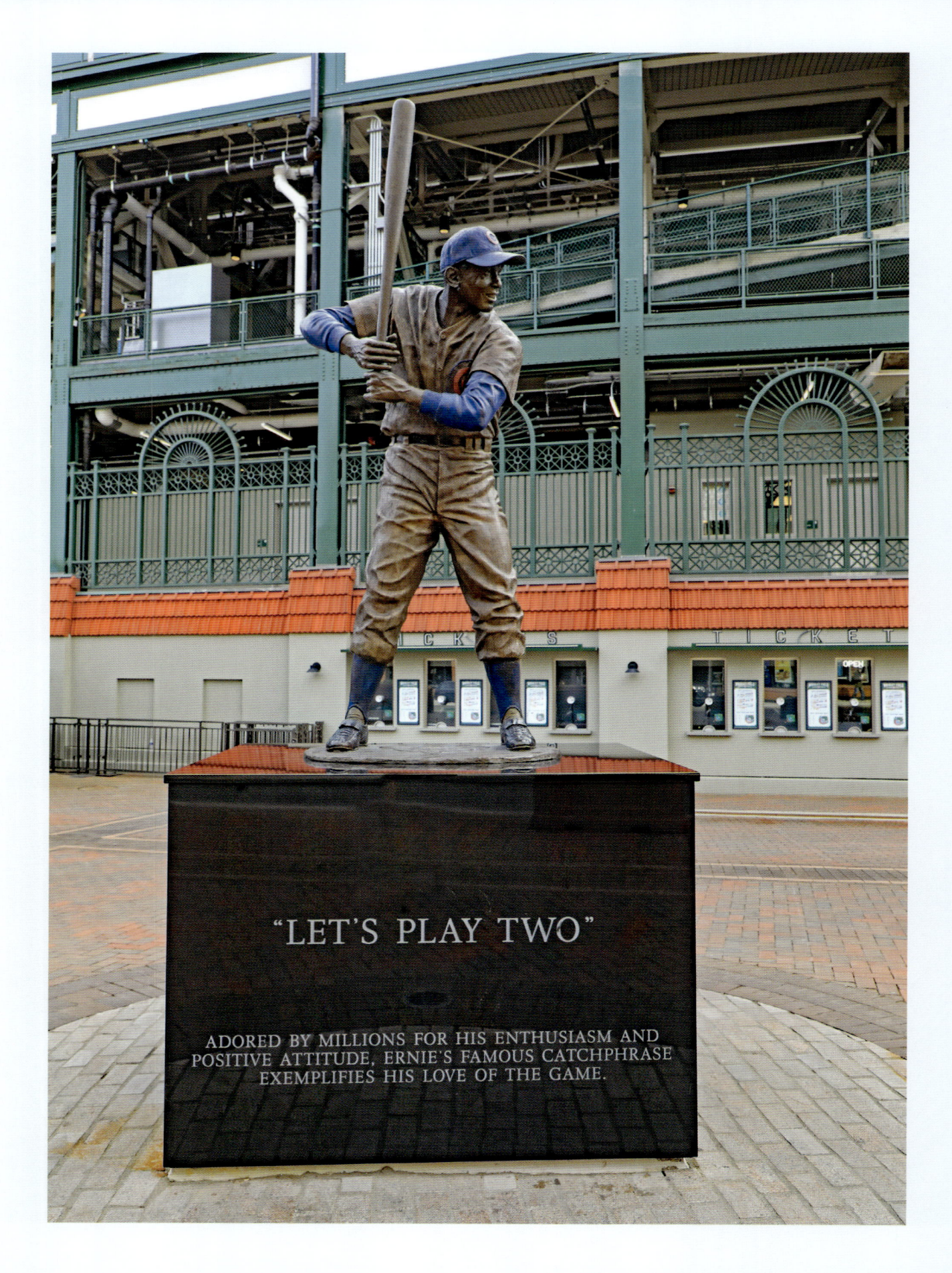

"LET'S PLAY TWO"

ADORED BY MILLIONS FOR HIS ENTHUSIASM AND POSITIVE ATTITUDE, ERNIE'S FAMOUS CATCHPHRASE EXEMPLIFIES HIS LOVE OF THE GAME.

Ernie Banks Statue *(opposite)*

"Let's play two," became Chicago Cubs player Ernie Banks' signature line. The statue was dedicated in 2008 and is a nod to the first Cubs player to have his number retired. "Mr. Cub" played 19 seasons, was a two-time National League MVP and was inducted into the Baseball Hall of Fame in 1977.

The Spirit *(top)*

"The best there ever was. The best there ever will be," are the words inscribed at the base of the 12-foot-tall bronze statue of Chicago Bulls legend Michael Jordan. Sculpted by Omri Amrany and Julie Rotblatt-Amrany, it was unveiled in 1994 and is the rallying point for fans any time the Bulls win.

United Center *(bottom)*

Opened in 1994 as the home of the Chicago Bulls and the Chicago Blackhawks, this multipurpose venue hosts more than 200 events a year. The largest arena in the United States, it has seating for 23,500 fans and has been nicknamed "The house that Michael Jordan built."

125

Chicago Botanic Garden *(top)*

Located 20 miles north of Chicago in Glencoe, the Chicago Botanic Garden is situated on 385 acres and features 27 gardens and four natural areas. Known as the "father of environmental science," this statue of Carolus Linnaeus by Robert Berks depicts Linnaeus reaching for a plant.

A Living Museum *(bottom)*

Created as a living plant museum in 1972, today the Chicago Botanic Garden is situated on and around nine islands and six miles of lake shoreline. With over one million visitors a year, it is dedicated to education and conservation, has earned a Gold LEED rating, and is considered a national leader in sustainability.

Cultivating Sustainability
(opposite top and bottom)

The garden's missionis to cultivate the power of plants to sustain and enrich life. The Buehler Enabling Garden (top) is a hands-on teaching garden that demonstrates that people of any physical ability can garden. Throughout the garden are 30 alluring pools and fountains.

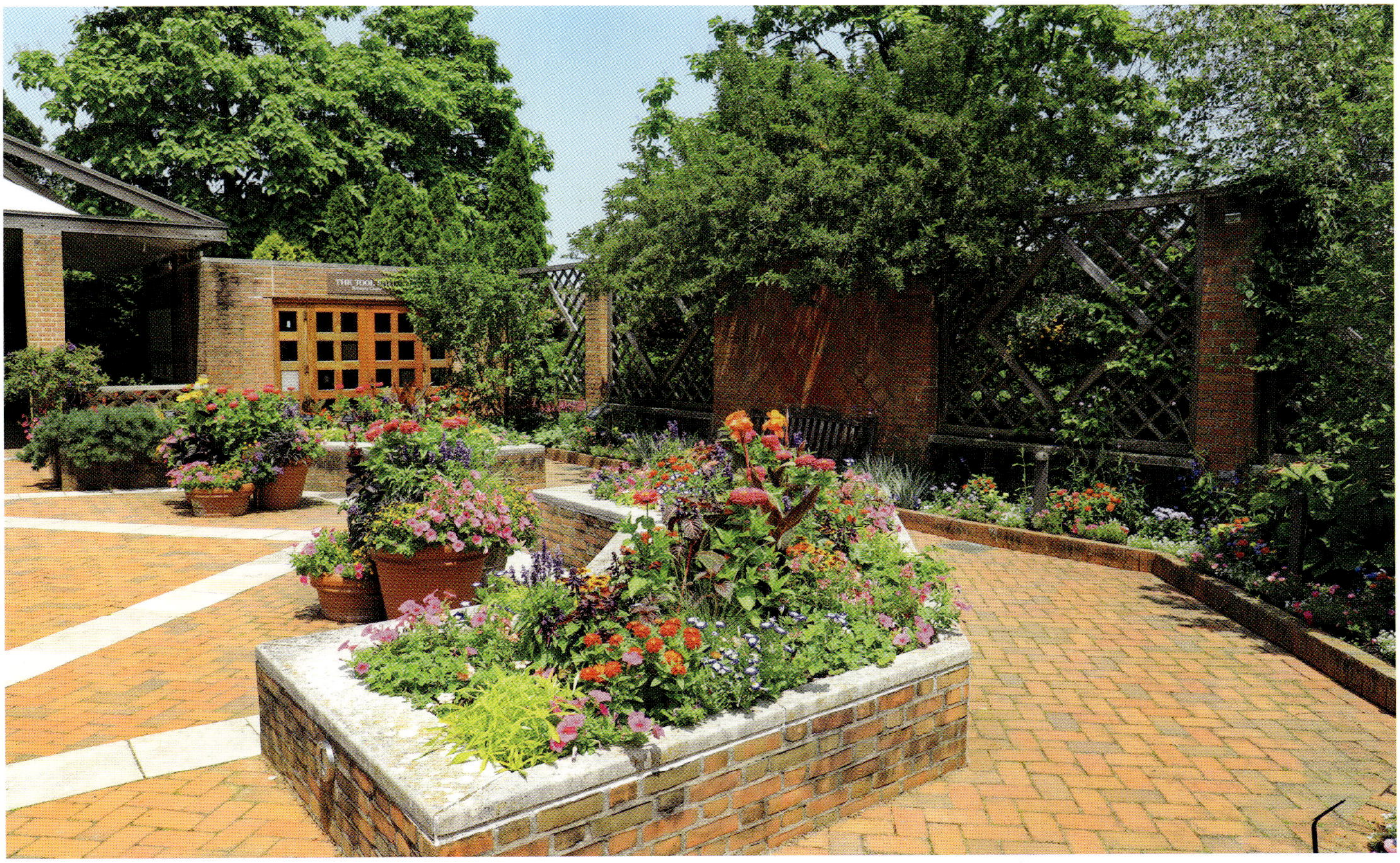

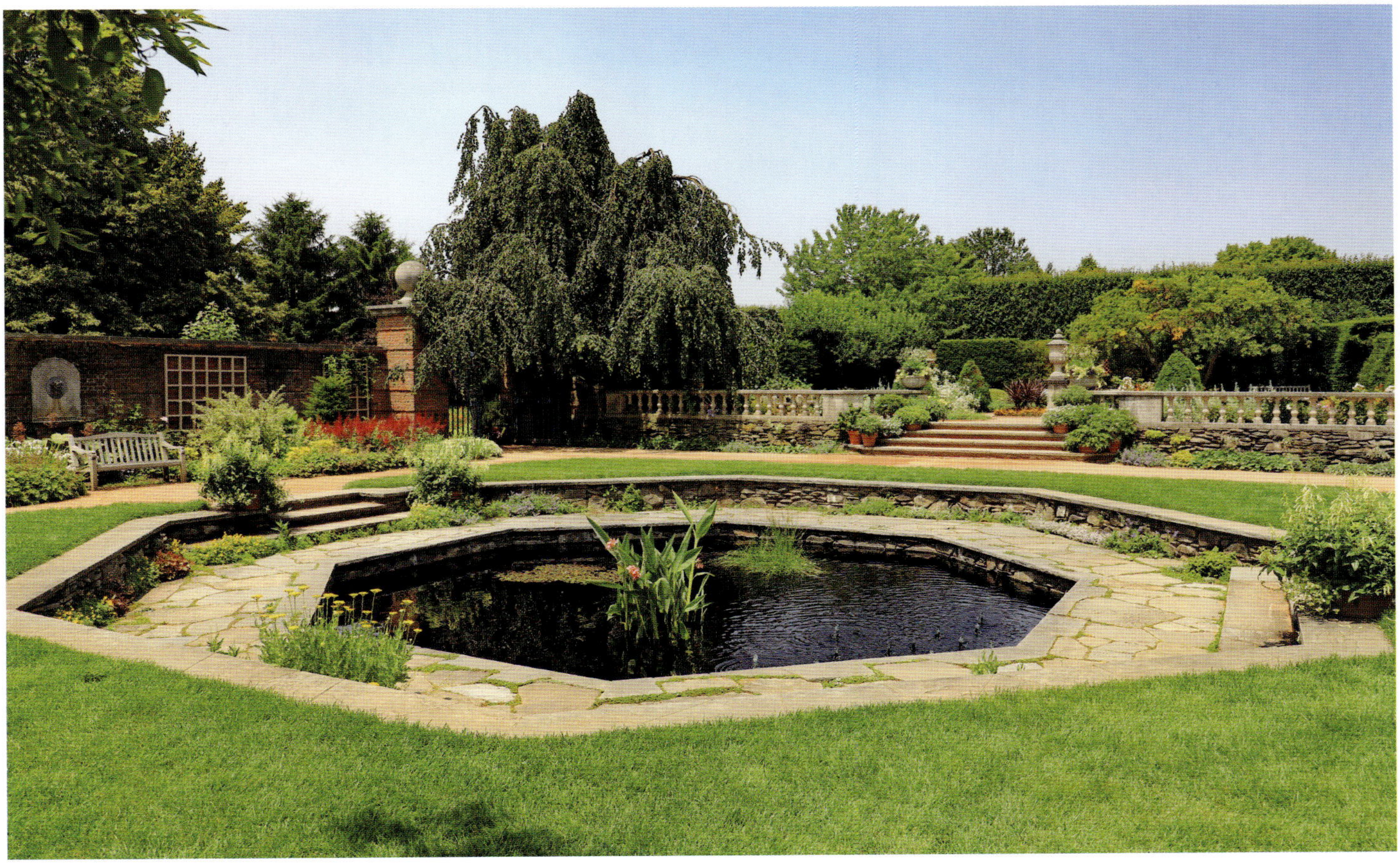

Tom Barrat is a photographer specializing in travel, wildlife, and architecture. He has a portfolio of digital images from all over the United States and 30 countries and is a contributing stock photographer to multiple stock agencies as well as his website. With over 60,000 images downloaded for use on websites, magazine ads, books, and other print media, over half are purchased and used internationally. He is a former executive in software development, Internet banking, and debit card processing. Tom worked with Twin Lights Publishers as the photographer for the very successful book, *Chicago, A Photographic Portrait II*, and is delighted to be working with them again for this publication. Tom and his wife lived in Chicago for eight years and visit Chicago often for business and to be with friends. Go to TomBarratPhotography.com to learn more about Tom.

Courtney Pitt was born and raised in the Chicagoland area. After she attended Boston University for journalism, Courtney moved back to Chicago to work in the magazine industry, where she has written for *Chicago Magazine* and *Chicago-Scene Magazine*. Her most recent job was publisher for *Chicago Woman Magazine*. Courtney is currently working on a series of historical novels set after the Revolutionary War. She enjoys doing historical research on America when it was a fledgling democracy. Courtney also devotes her free time to philanthropic efforts that help people in the city she loves. Courtney lives in downtown Chicago with her two wonderful daughters. For more information, email Courtney at Courtney@CourtneyPitt.com.